S0-CON-151

What's Your

What's Your Shine?
A Method for Discovering Who You Are
and Why It Matters

Copyright © 2020 by Claudia K. Beeny

All rights reserved. No part of this publication may be
reproduced, distributed, or transmitted in any form or
by any means, including photocopying, recording, or
other electronic or mechanical methods, without the prior
written permission of the publisher, except in the case of
brief quotations embodied in critical reviews and certain
other noncommercial uses permitted by copyright law.

ISBN: 978-0-578-61473-1

Published by CKB Group, LLC

Submit queries, including permissions requests
and requests for bulk orders, to the House of Shine at
info@houseofshine.com.

What's Your

Shine?

A METHOD *for* DISCOVERING
WHO YOU ARE *and* WHY IT MATTERS

Claudia Beeny Ph.D.

CONTENTS

INTRODUCTION

I clearly remember that light-bulb moment when I realized I loved the work I was doing and that I could spend the rest of my days helping others feel the same way. That day, I was sitting at the kitchen table in a home my family and I recently moved into, after moving across the country to accommodate my husband's job. I had a computer and journal open in front of me and a folder and cell phone to one side. The folder and phone were there because I had a phone interview scheduled later that morning. Twenty minutes later, to be exact. It was for a position commensurate with my twenty-five years of experience working in higher education. Landing this position would mean staying on my professional path; moving further up the ladder and retaining all those creature comforts that come with being a Ph.D. in the world of academia.

I had the computer and journal positioned directly in

front of me because at that moment I was deep in the middle of doing research; but not for the job. Responsible, professional me knew I should shut the journal and laptop and prepare for the interview that was getting closer by the minute. The nagging voice inside my head insisted I should be posing mock questions to myself, reviewing the online school paper for hot topics interviewers were sure to raise, or revisiting my résumé and cover letter to make sure no points they referenced would catch me off guard. Now there were only twelve minutes until the interview, and ambitious me knew there were things I should have been doing to prepare. But I wasn't doing any of them.

Instead, I was sitting at my computer completely engrossed in researching my blog topic for the following week. Inspired by World Kindness Day, I had wanted to feature an international idea-a-day about ways readers could spread a little kindness in their corner of the world. I researched how to say "You shine" in twenty or thirty languages. I explored the concept of pen pals, and paged through recipes for the favorite local baked treats from Germany to Jaipur. I looked into microlending programs for women around the world, and even contemplated featuring individual women who were busy spreading kindness in their respective communities. The plan was to travel virtually to a different country each day and celebrate kindness along the way.

Six minutes until the interview and I still couldn't get myself to break away.

Since I'd started the blog the year before, my readers had been slowly growing into a vibrant community, leading me to imagine how virtual passports could add an element of interest, and whether I should offer a prize or a patch to any reader who engaged all week. Patches were something I had introduced months earlier as a way of building identity, investment, and involvement among group members. In this case, my blog readers earned patches for completing activities, then sewed them onto old jeans or a favorite kitchen apron. The patches were a symbol of my bigger goal of building community through a series of shared experiences, so losing myself on a website stocked with different kinds of patches was like a kid getting lost in a candy store.

Two minutes until interview time.

Still scanning for patches.

One minute.

Still searching.

Brrrrrrng.

"Hello, this is Claudia…"

That's when the light bulb went on for me: Immediately after the interview ended I reopened my journal because I never wanted to forget the details of how I had spent this time, just minutes before a phone interview for a great job at a well-respected university. Instead of preparing to secure paid employment, I was working harder at my blog—something that wasn't paying work at all. It was a hobby; something I had started between jobs after my youngest son was born.

But I loved all aspects of this "hobby": looking out at the weeks ahead, using my creativity to program virtual experiences for people all over the United States and, eventually, perhaps, the world. This work drew on my particular combination of Strengths in a way that previous jobs hadn't and, deep down, I knew the prospective job at this new university wouldn't either. The truth is that I loved writing blog posts more than doing the job I was up for, and my behavior in the minutes leading up to the interview showed it.

Years earlier, after completing the CliftonStrengths test as part of a professional development series at the university where I was employed, I received my results in a report outlining my "Top Five Strengths", along with a short description of each. The descriptors of my Strengths made sense, and it was affirming to hear the facilitator explain that I had a unique combination of thoughts, feelings, and beliefs (as is the case for each of us). My Strengths were: Strategic, Achiever, Focus, Input, and Ideation. After taking all this in, I then did what so many people do: I filed these Strengths away in a drawer and went on doing what I do.

Until the morning of that interview.

That morning, I saw the five StrengthsFinder themes as puzzle pieces sliding perfectly into place. In that light-bulb moment, I realized exactly why I loved blogging as much as I did. First and foremost, the entire endeavor was a creative act of taking in information (Input), then transforming that information into tangible ideas (Ideation) that people could use to foster community in their corner of the world. Sequencing the ideas into theme weeks required planning (Strategic) and the goal of filling all fifty-two weeks with something different energized me (Focus). Keeping it going day after day, week after week, month after month, and, what turned into year after year, was an act of stamina—something a person with the Achiever theme has plenty of.

In retrospect, the process of understanding myself probably worked more like bringing the lights up slowly with a dimmer switch than snapping on a light all at once; this moment tipped off a gradual awakening rather than bringing about a sudden realization. It felt like a light-bulb moment, though, because my breakthrough had come about after a long period of quiet thinking and reflecting. As I look back fondly at those simpler days—when my only objectives were to generate ideas and write blog posts—three activities strike me as particularly important to nurturing that reflective process, and bringing on that light-bulb realization.

The first was making good use of my free time or "margin," as I like to call it. Most of us lead lives so packed with activity that we rarely take the time to stop and process how we feel about what we're doing. I was between jobs, so my schedule was more relaxed than normal and I had time to think about how I was spending my days. I was also driving my own schedule, which helped me notice which activities I was choosing to fill my days with, and which I avoided or didn't miss doing for work.

The second thing was making time to walk outside every day. Walking is something I have always enjoyed doing, but when life feels rushed, it's easy to believe you have to run, not walk, or, if you're really busy, skip exercise altogether. Those days, I usually left my house at noon and did a one-and-a-half-hour walk around a local park. I took the same route every day and I always went alone, without even a set of headphones. The familiarity of the route coupled with the quiet allowed new thoughts to seep into my mind. I began to notice patterns in my thinking, like how often I thought about people in my life who deserved recognition or creative activities I could do with my kids. I also thought about the aspects of my life with which I was satisfied and those with which I was dissatisfied. For example, I loved how balanced my life felt and how much better my perspective was about the little annoyances that in the past would have seemed big. But, I could also feel myself rejecting the loss of my identity and resenting the sacrifice I felt like I had made professionally by changing career paths after so many years of schooling.

Finally, I started journaling, and today I would probably describe this activity as the most important of the three. To be clear, before I started my blog, I had never been a person who journaled. Like so many, I had romanticized the idea of writing in a diary and, therefore, had many false starts. I bought journals expecting to write my deep, dark thoughts in them—using nothing but perfect penmanship—and after three or four days, the pressure would be too much and I would stop. The difference this time around was that I only journaled to capture blog post ideas or other creative ideas and initiatives that I didn't want to forget: I sketched messy pictures, jotted down favorite quotes, taped interesting advertisements to the pages, scribbled notes worth remembering from a TED Talk or blogger, and sometimes used it for the inane purpose of making to-do lists. This journaling was purely functional, but because I was filling the pages with things that inspired me, I loved having it with me and often sought reasons to fill its pages. Today, I also occasionally include in my journal the emotions around events going on in my life, but that's only because after so many years journaling has proven itself to be a trusted friend.

At House of Shine, we encourage people to record data about their Shine (strengths, hobbies, interests and irritants, needs, and life experiences) in dedicated journals, then synthesize this information and draw conclusions from it about everything from the work environment they would most enjoy, to patterns in their behavior, to simple likes and dislikes. Throughout this book, you'll see prompts for journaling and examples of how these types of notes have served others. To read more about how to start your "Shine Notes," see page 131.

One of the most instructive things I find about capturing aspects of my life on paper is the ability to go back years later and see what I considered noteworthy. What was I excited about? What was causing me stress? What was I noticing and daydreaming about? What ideas were consuming me? What books was I reading and what about them made me take notice? I like to think about my old entries relative to current-day entries and see which topics persist, notice if there are areas where I have grown, and see how seeds planted one year eventually manifested in an achievement years later. It was actually this type of reflection over time that eventually led to my aha moment at the kitchen table.

Once I understood my Strengths in action, as well as other interests and pastimes I came to believe were central to feeling fulfilled, I better understood why I loved blogging as much as I did. By extension, it meant I also better understood what it was about other jobs that I liked and disliked. Suddenly what seemed like a game of luck—*Will I like this job or not?*—became a process of analysis and discernment. That's when I realized for the first time that my feelings of energy, enthusiasm, passion, joy, and fulfillment were feelings anyone could have about their life. That is, provided they had useful information about themselves and understood how to apply it toward confident decision-making in the future.

That was more than a decade ago. Today, this hobby has become a full-time job running House of Shine, a nonprofit organization. House of Shine is built on the premise that there are contributions inside every person just waiting to be made; irresistible ways of using our talents and gifts that make us feel as motivated as I did while researching blog posts at my kitchen table. The evolution of our organization also worked more like gradually raising the lights with a dimmer switch: In the beginning, when my kids were little, I asked their teachers if I could use a class period to facilitate an activity with their classmates—an experience reinforcing for them that each student was born with talents and gifts. As my children advanced grades, I created more content and, slowly, the Shine philosophy became more formalized.

Years working in higher education convinced me that most students did not arrive on campus knowing how to build lives around the kind of work that tapped into their unique combination of talents and gifts. In fact, most students had no idea what their talents and gifts might be. Worse yet, I was doing leadership development for employees at my husband's business, and most of these seasoned professionals had also devoted precious little time to thinking about who they were and how they could use what they knew about themselves to optimize the life they were living. Throw on top of that a large network of moms clamoring for the same kinds of insights and information. For many of these women, their days were spent tending to their families, with little time spent thinking about talents, preferences, interests, or needs. Yet sparks of passion would be ignited whenever the spotlight was turned on these individuals long enough to illuminate these otherwise-forgotten personal insights. All told, from K-12 student to college student to seasoned professional to busy mom, it was the contributions waiting to be made that lay dormant inside each of these people that motivated me to keep growing House of Shine. This is my motivation, too, in writing this book—to help you unearth and polish your Shine.

This book is designed to spark and guide a conversation between you and you. It is a framework that helps shine a light on answers to two big questions that most of us grapple with throughout life: *Who am I?* and *Why does it matter who I am?* The Shine framework presented in the pages that follow is simple and straightforward, because when you are quiet and when you know what you are listening for, living a happy and fulfilling life does not have to be complicated. It might require some work. It might require courage. But it does not have to be complicated. In fact, my experience tells me the closer you get to living your purpose, the more light there is, the more clarity you gain on priorities, and the clearer everything else appears.

Admittedly, not everyone reading this book is starting at the same place. Some of us grew up in difficult and dark family situations, which caused emotional pain that we're still trying to resolve. Others are living under the looming cloud of health or financial problems and the idea of living a fulfilling life might strike you as a luxury you can't afford. As humans, though, most of us are hardwired to want to improve our conditions, and it's that glimmer of hope or simple aspiration for more than you presently have that this book seeks to connect with.

Lastly, I see a need for a worldview focused more on what is right than what is wrong, focused more on what we have than what we don't, and focused more on what is good than what is bad. I see a place where people are too satisfied living their own purpose to needlessly bully or make life difficult for another person. I see a world where students show up to school eager to learn because they understand gaining knowledge on a range of subjects can be interesting when it's linked to their self-knowledge. I see a world where parents worry less about engineering achievements for their kids and more about carving out free time so boredom can evolve into curiosity, then exploration. I see a world where leaders imagine every room they enter as a vault of talent and see their job as choreographing diverse talents in such a way that the whole they envision is always greater than the sum of people's individual parts. I see communities where members scan their environment for what is needed and immediately get busy thinking about how what they possess could be useful to someone else. And lastly, I see you: I see you with all of your talents and gifts, with your quirky likes and dislikes, and your unique experiences, woven together into a one-of-a-kind person placed here on earth to make contributions that are also, in turn, one of a kind.

The following pages are the result of more than ten years of passionate work on this subject. The book is organized into five concise chapters. Chapter 1 sets the groundwork, discussing why knowing yourself and making your own unique contribution is so important. I will touch on the increasingly noisy world we live in and the benefits of mobilizing people's talents and interests for the greater good. Chapters 2, 3, and 4 are titled "Be," "Do," and "Share," respectively. Each contains a piece of the framework we use at House of Shine when teaching people of all ages how to understand what living a fulfilling life means to them.

Chapter 2, "Be," focuses on self-discovery. It uses each letter of the word "shine" to help readers revisit things about themselves they might have forgotten or never recognized as important. "Do," the third chapter, presents ideas for strengthening our innate skills and attributes, much like we would use a gym to strengthen our physical bodies. And Chapter 4, "Share," provides examples of five people at various stages of their lives who are living fulfilling lives through the application of our Shine framework. This chapter answers the question "What do I do from here?" by way of introducing readers to Shineology—a term we have come up with to emphasize the ongoing importance of studying self and using what we know to craft fulfilling lives no matter what stage of life we are in.

CHAPTER 1

Sshhhh. . . Quiet

I woke up this morning to the alarm on my iPhone. Then I traipsed into the kitchen, brewed a cup of coffee with my Keurig, and sat down at my computer to continue working on this book. I love technology and all the convenience that comes from electronic appliances. I love the hair dryer I use every morning, the microwave that heats up my morning oatmeal, the TV I tune in to while getting dressed, the car that transports my kids to school, and the Waze app that assures I don't get lost while driving to a client appointment. I am a proponent of modern technology and all the ways it makes my life easier.

And still. . .

It is hard not to be a little jealous of how quiet the world was when my parents and their parents were growing up.

Today, in part due to automation and advances in technology, noise is everywhere. Even as I type, alone in my house, the hum of the refrigerator is in the background and the air conditioning just kicked on. When it comes to almost everything we do, the world has become a noisier place.

Take communication, for example. Gone are the days when communicating with someone at a distance was done by quietly sitting down to write a letter. Eventually the simplicity of paper and pen or the typewriter was replaced with the more advanced telegram. Then came the telephone, and though not everyone had one in the beginning, those who did introduced a whole new sound into their homes: the ringing telephone. Eventually phones were ringing in every home and went from rotary to push button, the technology advancing quickly. Eventually cordless phones presented the added convenience of taking our conversations from one room of our home to another. By the 70s, we had the first mobile phones and when those became small and affordable enough, conversations that were normally confined to our homes or offices could now take place in the streets. Now everyone, whether we wanted to or not, got to experience the noise generated by other people's telephones. Today, of course, our phones are handheld computers capable of doing so much more than just making phone calls. And with every new bell and whistle offered comes more noise.

The same is true of transportation. When my parents' parents were young, walking was their primary mode of transportation. I imagine they traveled long stretches where the only sounds heard were of wildlife or the wind rustling through trees. Then came horses and carts, then bicycles, trains, cars, planes, and even rockets. Somewhere in all of that we learned how to wire our cars with audio equipment, assuring that even if we were traveling solo, it wouldn't have to be in solitude. Today in an almost poetic turn of events, we can use our hand-held devices to summon and pay for an Uber driver to give us a ride in a car that is probably playing music. And we can do all of it without having to utter a word. On the one hand automation and technology has made our world a noisier place, and on the other, the old-fashioned sounds of people interacting are becoming harder and harder to find.

> ## We have grown accustomed to constant noise in the background and foreground of our lives.

Recently, I visited a spa with girlfriends and we couldn't help but smile at the custom-printed sleeping bags the spa employee issued us for our phones. "Give your technology a rest this weekend" was the message being communicated by the spa. Perhaps even more noteworthy than this was the idea that the four of us needed to reserve a weekend and pay for peace and quiet. But that is what happened. We met up for dinner each evening, but during the day we tucked ourselves away in different nooks and crannies of the property, savoring the break from our noisy everyday lives.

Visual Noise

Noise doesn't stop at what surrounds us audibly. There is also visual noise—the material items surrounding us that create so much additional distraction we have a hard time hearing ourselves think. Most of us could look up from reading right now and spot a countertop in our home or office that perfectly illustrates this point. Stacks of paper to be tossed or filed; a stack of materials necessary to complete an unfinished project; the unfinished project itself; a recently gifted trinket, awaiting a decision about where it goes; and the countless other insidious items that work their ways into our lives. This is the visual noise that operates like an annoying buzz in our ears; a forever reminder that there is more: More to do; more to manage; more to think about.

On a trip to Italy a few years ago, my family and I saw Michelangelo's breathtaking sculpture, the *David*. Our tour guide brought the sculpture to life by filling our minds with interesting facts about how long it took to make, why it was commissioned, how tall the work of art stood, and how much it weighed. To me, the most interesting tidbit our guide shared was that the *David* is carved from a single block of marble. She quoted Michelangelo as saying, "Every block of stone has a statue inside it and it is the task of the sculptor to discover it. I saw the angel in the marble and carved until I set him free."

The image of Michelangelo chiseling away at the block of marble until the masterpiece within it could be revealed captured my attention and left me thinking about other applications of this approach. I wondered what would happen if we lived in a world where, rather than feeling as though to be admired we needed more material things, we could find our confidence in having less. Less clothing, fewer gadgets, smaller homes. Less clothing could simplify morning decision making. Fewer gadgets provide fewer distractions. And smaller homes require less time-consuming maintenance. The simplicity of less leads to greater clarity of thought in the same way less overgrowth in the garden lets you see the beauty of each flower or less background noise allows you to hear each instrument in an ensemble. Or a less verbose sentence, void of all the same overused and redundant words, allows readers who might be sitting and reading *this* sentence to understand the circuitous route I am dragging them through to make a relatively simple point.

I felt myself challenged by this notion when I returned home from our trip and entered my closet to unpack my bags. Immediately I was faced with a wall stocked full of pants—something I've always acquired a lot of. If I was going on a date and wanted to feel confident, new jeans could do the trick. If I was nervous about an upcoming keynote, a new pair of trousers was the magic confidence-building item that I needed to believe I would make a good impression. The right pants could even ward off catty judgments from a new social circle of girlfriends. Every uncertainty, insecurity, or apprehension was fixed with a new pair of pants, which I guess is how I eventually ended up with seventy-eight pairs hanging in my closet. (Yes, really.) My experience with Michelangelo's sculpture made me realize that the pants were just noise. They were noise I hung in my closet to help drown out the inner critic who never stops chastising me about my chunky legs. Paring away the excess pairs of pants from my collection was like quieting the orchestra's accompaniment until the only thing left was the simple sound of the soloist's melody. I found my inner critic had been exposed: This was music to my ears and exactly what I needed to see and think more clearly.

What whittling down my collection to far fewer pairs of pants did for me was to visually simplify so that I could clearly see why I had made the decisions that I did. Seeing my reduced wardrobe, I wondered why I had started accumulating clothes like that; was it boredom, vanity, addiction, power, control? I came to know that in my case, it was insecurity. I grew up in a house with two very lean sisters and a mother who was never really satisfied with her own body. I internalized messaging around me that slender legs are better than full legs and have spent the rest of my life coming up with strategies for either compensating or hiding this thing about myself that I dislike. It's resulted in missed experiences, wasted energy, and, of course, a lot of extra expense.

How about you? If you scrutinize the excess in your life, whether it be of material things like clothes, technology, and books, or excessive food consumption, what can you learn about the noise it provides? What issue is this noise drowning out for you and how might your life be better and more peaceful if you got clear on the real issue at hand?

Mental Exhaustion

The inner critic, like modern-day noise, is a little like the sun in how pervasive and omnipresent it is. On a brilliant, clear day, the sun is intense, following you and pressing down on your skin until you apply sunscreen or you take cover inside. On a cloudier day, the effects of the sun might be less obvious, but public service announcements help us understand that even with the dimmer sunlight, harmful ultraviolet rays are still penetrating our skin. The same is true of noise. Most of us understand the damaging effects of attending a loud rock concert, but we are less likely to see the detrimental effects of exposing ourselves to a steady stream of email or text notifications, background noise from the TV, or excess items stacked up on our counters and in our closets. In both cases, the best solution for managing sun and noise is moderation; knowing how much exposure to get before the effects are detrimental.

Constant noise requires that we constantly process, but our brains need rest just like our bodies. Imagine waking up and immediately hitting the floor to do one hundred pushups. Then downstairs to breakfast, but instead of sitting and easing into your day with eggs and bacon, you had to eat breakfast while running in place. Then you would do lunges while walking back upstairs, laps through the shower, a long jump back downstairs, a full sprint to work, and then a long marathon, with no stopping until the workday is done. Then you'd sprint back home, do dips through dinner, and reps on the stair-climber before finally stretching out in bed. Every muscle in your body would be exhausted and everyone you knew would understand why. Why then do we have such a hard time acknowledging that noise all day is also exhausting?

In fact, in many ways it seems there is a deliberate infusion of noise from companies seeking to capture and keep our attention. Watches used to be quiet, but now they have alarms and can play music. Clothing stores didn't always blast music to attract young shoppers, but somewhere along the line, loud music became a necessity. Greeting cards sing, stuffed animals talk, and bells and buzzers let us know that appliances are working (or not). Even the gadgets manufactured to make noise want us to make noise, too. Alexa and Siri are happy to chime in on our dinner table conversation, but only after we talk to them first. If all of this isn't proof enough that the world is becoming a noisier place, then we must only take look at the noise-canceling industry that is popping up around us. Headphones, sleep machines, and noise-canceling curtains are just a few examples of measures we've taken to reclaim some of the quiet lost through the adoption of automation and technology. Ask anyone trying to produce a podcast outside of a recording studio and they'll tell you how hard it is to find quiet.

You'd think there would be more ardent ambassadors for quiet considering all the accomplished people who either savored quiet or sang its praises. Charles Dickens walked for miles in quiet, using the time to make observations of different scenes and to develop his classic stories. Successful businessman and billionaire Warren Buffett proudly attributes much of his success to the quiet time he sets aside daily for thinking. Artist Georgia O'Keeffe retreated to northern

New Mexico for long spells so she could paint in quiet. Jerry Seinfeld, best known for making people laugh uproariously, meditates regularly. And athletes Tiger Woods and Serena Williams have what sports psychologists call the "quiet eye"—a technique to hone the ability to block out distracting noise during competitions.

Each of these superstars in their respective fields learned the power of cultivating quiet. They each also—and not coincidentally—have a high degree of self-awareness that has allowed them to connect with and maximize their unique combination of strengths.

A Case for Self-Awareness

It takes a great deal of self-awareness and a strong sense of personal responsibility to identify foundational moments in our lives, and then understand how they connect to a series of other such moments. Yet seeing and understanding those connections can prove crucial to happiness, success, and fulfillment, helping us reconcile the past while also shaping our future decision making. For instance, one foundational moment in my life dates back to my first day of fourth grade at a new school. My well-intended teacher tried to welcome me into the classroom community by selecting me to answer a question to which I did not know the answer. I vividly remember sitting in my seat, paralyzed with fear, feeling like an hour ticked by before she finally decided to call on another student. That moment is foundational because it evoked a powerful emotion in me, one that I've come to recognize at various other points in my life. I felt it the time I scored a basket for the wrong team; when I skipped a fraternity party in college because I didn't think I had the right outfit to wear; or when I sat out countless dances after someone *kindly* pointed out that I had no rhythm. Developing self-awareness helped me realize that I am painfully self-conscious and that, over the years, I have allowed a fear of rejection and ridicule to keep me from making memories with people I care about. What personal responsibility does for me is place a spotlight on the issue so I can confront my underlying fears and stop allowing important moments to pass me by.

With so much riding on self-awareness, it is interesting that most institutions don't pay it more attention. Instead, we as a society think of self-awareness as something that just comes naturally with the maturation process and assume that eventually everyone will live long enough to learn their likes and dislikes. We believe this process will implicitly happen, rather than expecting leaders to facilitate experiences that make self-knowledge explicit.

Growing up, our education (in
school and life) largely focuses
on things outside ourselves, yet
it is self-inquiry that nets the greatest
gains in terms of happiness, satisfaction, and meaningful contributions to
the world.

In schools, we rally around character education lessons, ignoring the fact that risk-taking, for instance, looks very different for an introverted child than it does for an extroverted child. Or that resilience, depending on life experiences, can take very different forms. So while yes, character traits are important, it is the awareness of how those traits are applied that helps a student effectively integrate them into his or her life.

The same is true in the workplace. We expect students to move through an educational system that doesn't explicitly teach self-awareness, then graduate from college or a trade school ready to make a meaningful contribution in the workforce. We want employees to collaborate, take initiative, and play well with others, but we never stop to think who along the way was responsible for making self-knowledge as easy to access as, say, the internet. Instead, dissatisfied employers and employees keep searching externally for the kind of harmony that most often comes from within.

The fact is, self-awareness has probably never been harder to come by than it is today. The barrage of noise surrounding us makes it virtually impossible to hear ourselves think. If our cell phone isn't ringing, then we are getting email, sending texts, or checking out how we stack up against our friends on Facebook, Instagram, or Pinterest. Even if quiet wasn't the hot commodity it has become, there's another limited resource that is essential to self-awareness: time for reflection. We even resort to downloading meditation apps on our phones so, ironically, we can break from the noise around us and go through the difficult paces of "thinking" about nothing.

Unlike meditation, where we might sit quietly and use self-discipline to think about nothing, the act of becoming self-aware requires both active participation and plenty of thought.

With more noise and less time
for reflection, it has never been
more important to intentionally
create space for discovering who we
are and why it matters.

Listening for You

Of all the reasons to seek and savor quiet, the most important is to hear your Inner Voice. You were born to shine, using your unique set of talents and gifts.

You were born to contribute to this world in a way that is different from anyone else and the nature of those contributions is deeply embedded in the unique combination of talents and gifts with which you were born.

But what *are* your unique talents and gifts and how do you determine how you're supposed to deploy them? That's the tricky part; these are the questions so many of us have trouble answering. Yet finding the answers is worth the effort, because as human beings, our feelings of happiness and fulfillment are connected to knowing we matter and that we are part of something bigger than ourselves.

It would be so much easier if we came with a set of instructions like a new appliances purchased from a store. Our parents could file our manual away until we were old enough to read it and then, when the time was right, we could pore over the pages in search of answers to exactly how we work best, and what our true vocation is. Or, like a page out of Harry Potter, maybe we could sit on a stool and have a Sorting Hat placed upon our heads. Then a voice would ring out and magically tell us about our destiny. But we don't come with an instruction manual and the Sorting Hat is fiction, so each of us is left to our own devices to understand for ourselves who we are, and why who we are matters.

Fortunately, there *is* something we are all given: It's that voice inside our head; the one I referenced earlier that was chastising me about my legs. The real job of the Inner Voice, though, is much more constructive and important than providing negative criticism. Its real job is to guide us along our path of self-discovery; to lead us to the crossroads of our innate talents and the purposes we can best serve throughout our lifetime. In fact, when we are busy listening to our Inner Voice for all the right reasons, what we often notice is that the sounds of insecurity and negativity get drowned out.

The problem with so much noise competing for our attention is it can make it hard to hear what the Inner Voice is trying to say. And like anyone who wants to be heard but feels ignored, eventually the voice will give up and go away (or start to sound like that negative inner critic). When we lose that guidance, we become less clear about what we like and don't like, when we're having fun and when we feel sapped of energy, what our preferences are, and when we last felt real joy and fulfillment. Our Inner Voice doesn't pick up and leave in a huff; it's a much subtler fading away, and we know it's happened when one day turns into two, then three, then a week, then a month, and a year, and then five years, and suddenly we look around and wonder how so much time passed and none of the hopes and dreams we initially had for ourselves came to pass.

Preventing the voice from disappearing, or summoning its return, doesn't have to be difficult. I like to think of it as a daily phone call I have with myself; a conversation between me and me. Sometimes the conversation happens in the car on my way home from dropping the boys at school, at other times while taking a walk by myself or drying my hair. Conversation is easy, because I find the Inner Voice[1] to be curious and responsive: It wants to know all sorts of things, such as when during the day I feel strongest; what am I doing and with whom am I doing it? It wants to know all about how I like to spend my free time and what clues my hobbies can provide me about my innate talents. The Inner Voice asks about the topics that interest me, but it's also really curious about the encounters I have during the day that rile me up and leave me

---

1 The Inner Voice is different from the Inner Critic. The Inner Critic also holds court inside our heads and for many it may feel as though the Critic is with us all day from waking to sleeping, using a megaphone to broadcast every last imperfection we see in ourselves. The good news is that both have volume knobs. Our goal then is to learn how to turn down the volume on our Inner Critic so we can more easily hear the instructive questions coming from our more constructive Inner Voice.

feeling discontented. These, too, I am learning from, as my Inner Voice offers important insights into how I can use my talents to help the greater good. It wants to hear me process whether the choices I am making are meeting my needs; more importantly, my Inner Voice has helped me realize it's OK for me to have needs and that my needs might be very different from those of other people in my life. I even rely on my Inner Voice to do things such as coach me through a difficult but necessary conversation in which I must speak up on behalf of a need I have that is not being met. And finally, my Inner Voice loves reflecting with me on experiences I have had. Did I like it? If so, why? Would I do it again or what might it mean moving forward?

It rained all day yesterday, and while I don't love how rainy days keep me from doing outdoor activities I love, I welcome them as opportunities to do other things I enjoy. I can get lost for hours cleaning out drawers, reorganizing closets, doing laundry, reading, writing in my journal, or exploring a topic on the internet. My husband is wired differently. Not only is he extroverted, gaining energy through his interactions with others, but he also needs a certain amount of physical activity and external stimulus to get motivated. Rainy days, therefore, leave him feeling sedentary and stir-crazy. What this means is that every twenty minutes or so, he's on my heels asking what I want to do next. My inside voice wants to whip around and scream, "Exactly what I am doing right now! I am perfectly content, you're the one who's bored!" On a bad day, my exasperation can send me into a downward spiral where I am projecting ahead to our twilight years and panicking that I'll never have uninterrupted alone time. Times like those are exactly when I rely on my Inner Voice to coach me through a constructive conversation about my need to be alone, while taking into account my desire to be a good companion. But void of hearing my Inner Voice and knowing I have legitimate needs that are different than those of my loved ones, I could run the risk of sacrificing my needs and wants in the short term and end up with feelings of resentment in the long term.

Our Inner Voice wants to know all of that and more. All we have to do is be willing to engage with it. The major challenge, though, is noise.

We were born in noisy houses;

On noisy streets;

In noisy towns;

In noisy cities;

In noisy countries;

In a noisy, noisy world.

Through all of that, the phone is ringing and our Inner Voice is calling. *Pick up the phone.* The rest of this book will show you how.

This phone icon indicates questions or suggestions for reflection:

(And you can learn more about the weekly—or even daily— phone conversations we at House of Shine encourage people to have between their head and heart in "DO52: A Weekly Phone Call Between Your Head and Your Heart" on page 92.)

CHAPTER 2

Be

"Be" is part one of the three-part Shine Method for discovering who you are and why who you are matters. It is the part of the process most focused on self-exploration, because if the end goal is to live a happy and contented life, we must first know who we are, what we care about, and how we might harness our energy to do something we will find fulfilling.

The S-H-I-N-E Framework

If you want to be a master at anything, a good place to start is to watch what the best of the best are already doing. Sports analysts do this when they add their expert commentary to slow-motion footage of a pro golfer's swing or the stroke of an Olympic swimmer. English professors do this when they analyze the works of history's most celebrated writers. Cookbooks provide lists of ingredients and step-by-step instructions already proven successful by a baker or chef. Couldn't this type of analysis also be useful for understanding the process involved in building a purposeful and fulfilled life? If we understand the thoughts, feelings, and behaviors associated with fulfilled people from all walks of life, couldn't we learn some strategies for crafting inspired lives of our own?

Notice that I said, "from all walks of life." This is because images promoted by modern media make it easy for us to confuse words such as "happy," "fulfilled," and "successful" with "famous." At House of Shine, we ardently believe that the best of the best can be found at every level of every industry, in every classroom of every school, and on every street of every neighborhood.

Excellence knows no bounds
and because it doesn't, if we're
looking through our Shine lens,
we can spot it everywhere and we can
teach it to everyone.

The Yellow Envelope Project is an initiative sponsored by House of Shine to support this very belief. This simple concept encourages participants to send letters of gratitude to people who shine in their corner of the world; everyday people like your morning barista, a thoughtful neighbor, star student, motivating manager, or the mail carrier who shows up to your house six days a week. In the ten years since we mailed the first letters, we have collected useful information about the recipients. We've learned about their backgrounds, what motivates them, and which of the qualities they possess that stand out to others.

In some ways, this book is a look at what we've learned. It's analyzing the slow-motion footage of what makes a Little League coach shine brighter than his peers or how a local florist stands out above the rest. It's an analysis of what makes an inspired teacher tick and why some volunteers add more value than highly paid employees. It is the book of recipes—including ingredients and steps—from joyful people living fulfilling lives.

Shine Grammar

At House of Shine we use the word "shine" as a verb, an adjective, and a noun. Understanding all three forms is important as we will use them interchangeably throughout this book. Earlier I said our framework "helps shine a light." That's "shine" being used as a verb. When we use the word as an adjective, we might say someone is a shining example of a positive attribute such as "grateful" or "courageous." Finally, we also use "shine" as a noun, when it denotes the bright quality something acquires when light is reflected from it. We believe a person's life can shine; to us, this means the person has done the hard work of unearthing her talents and gifts—letting them see the light of day—and then figuring out how to use them to make the world a better and brighter place. I guess you could say people who shine, shine their light in some corner of the world, thereby making the world a shinier place to live.

The process begins with self-awareness, but it wasn't until I experienced a realization on a plane trip many years ago that the concept of self-awareness became clear enough to me that I could, in turn, explain it to someone else. I was staring out the window with my journal and pen in hand. My thoughts were floating somewhere between whatever project I was working on at the time and the big dreams I was conjuring for House of Shine. I doodled the word "shine" down the left-hand side of my page and then effortlessly, as though my hand was working of its own free will, jotted the words:

- Strengths
- Hobbies
- Interests
- Needs
- Experiences

Whether they were born of my subconscious thoughts about the many Yellow Envelope recipients we'd met to date or something more mystical, I realized that those five words represented the information I considered essential for an individual making strong and confident decisions about his or her life. Since I first jotted them down all those years ago I've only made one change, adding a second word to the letter "I"— irritants. I thought about all the people I had met along the way who were motivated to make their corner of the world better because they were irritated. They had been irritated by the way someone they loved was being treated or by a process they believed was antiquated, or by a void that wasn't being filled. In fact, it seemed to me that a lot of significant contributions were the result of someone, somewhere being bothered by something. (More on that in a minute.)

All of that said, let's walk through each of these words and learn how you can use the S-H-I-N-E Method to tap into your unique combination of talents and gifts.

S = Strengths

My friend loves telling a story about the summer we lived together during college. She was a straight-A student in an accounting class and I was an average student taking a required economics class. At night we would hunker down and study in different parts of the house where we were living. I sat at the kitchen table and Shay usually studied in her bedroom. Shay knew me more as her former resident assistant, always planning floor activities, than as a studious junior trying to knock out required classes. She reminds me often about the evening she stopped by the kitchen table to cheer on all the focused studying I seemed to be doing and instead found me working intently on assembling a vision board. The allure of dreaming about my future while also assembling something creative far outweighed the importance I placed on mastering concepts of supply and demand.

I share that story not because I am proud of shirking my studies, but more because it illustrates the irresistible nature of engaging with our strengths. When we are doing something for which we have natural-born talents and gifts, not only do we look for reasons to do it, but time flies while we're absorbed in the task. You will see it in the imaginative teacher who gets lost in redecorating her classroom to support the new unit her students are starting. You'll see it in the detail-oriented assistant who meticulously organizes his office space. You'll see it in the confident networker who feels exhilarated each and every time she makes a sales call. I even see it in my twelve-year old son who will forgo playtime with neighborhood kids if it means he can spend a few more minutes experimenting with a recipe in the kitchen.

The Shine philosophy is in part built on the Strengths movement introduced by Gallup in 2001. Their well-studied belief is that each of us has patterns in the way we think, feel, and behave. We are born with these patterns and when we feed them with skills and knowledge, they grow even stronger. In fact, the more we feed our Strengths, the more we can rely on them to show up in times of need. That's what makes for an elite athlete. She might be born with aptitudes, but it is repeatedly feeding those natural aptitudes with knowledge and skills that increases the likelihood she will consistently perform well in competition.

None of us is born to be good at everything, which is all the more reason that discovering our innate talents and gifts is so important.

For example, no matter how many people encourage the elite athlete to become a motivational speaker, if her natural ways of thinking, feeling, and behaving don't lend themselves to speaking in front of large groups, sharing personal stories, organizing her thoughts, or traveling frequently, the chances of her becoming great at it are slim. She might get incrementally better through practice and observation, but she will never enjoy speaking to large groups and, therefore, it will never be something she is great at.

While emphasizing your strengths is not an excuse for shirking responsibilities associated with things that don't come naturally, focusing on your strengths can be helpful when deciding where to best invest limited resources of time and energy. For example, feelings of dread wash over me any time I have to troubleshoot problems with my computer. As a working person in the twenty-first century, I must be proficient enough at using technology that it does not get in the way of me doing my job. On the other hand, when choosing career paths, I wouldn't knowingly pursue technology-based jobs where proficiency is expected. That kind of position would leave me feeling weak on most workdays, and our goal is to seek experiences that leave us feeling strong.

What does make me feel strong is taking in new information, then distilling it into central themes I can teach others. I first remember experimenting with these natural inclinations when my best friend Laura and I used my father's blue books to play school as nine-year-olds. When I got older, I pored over magazines, looking at advertisements and deciding what made them catchy. Little did I know I would use what I learned years later when, as an RA, I trained other students how to create eye-catching promotions for their campus events. Fast-forward twenty years, and I was still finding ways to gather and disseminate information through daily blog posts—the cumulative effect of which set today's House of Shine in motion. The context and content evolved through the years, but my contribution has always revolved around my love of collecting information and synthesizing it in such a way that I could teach it to others.

The irony of strengths is that the essence of what it means to have a strength is the very thing that makes these unique ways of thinking, feeling, and behaving so hard to spot in ourselves. We look around and can't imagine that everyone else doesn't find those same tasks easy, so we dismiss what we do as nothing special. It wasn't until I was in my mid-thirties that I understood why friends always called me for gift or packaging ideas or why I instinctively distilled everything I learned into small teachable nuggets. Now that I am self-aware enough to recognize my strengths in action, I understand why Shay caught me creating something when I was supposed to be studying as well as how building a platform like House of Shine was a completely natural thing for me to do.

The same is true of you. What is something you are good at and enjoy doing, but that you've been surprised to learn is hard for others? Can you see how you've used that strength in a number of different settings over your lifetime? And if you are not currently using this strength, what one change could you make in your life that would allow you to exercise this talent?

H = Hobbies

There are 168 hours in a week, no more and no less. From the busiest CEO to the laziest teenager, we all have access to that same number of hours. It's what we choose to do with this time that is of interest to those of us seeking greater self-awareness and assurance that we are on the right path (and clues to how to change our path if we're not).

Hobbies are things we do in our free time. Ostensibly they are activities we enjoy doing enough that, given the opportunity, we will prioritize them over and above other things. Some of my hobbies include reading, journaling, taking long walks, playing board games, and listening to music while cleaning some portion of my house. No doubt there are readers who would consider my hobbies repentance for some terrible deed committed in a former life, in exactly the same way I don't understand my husband's love for swimming, biking, and running long distances or my neighbor's obsession with golf. Lesson number one about hobbies is they need not sound like fun to anyone but you.

Hobbies provide clues to our natural inclinations.

However, rather than focus on the activities themselves, it can be far more instructive to look at the similarities among our hobbies. A deeper look into my hobbies reveals for instance a penchant for being alone and having quiet time. Knowing this truth about myself, and having others know that about me, is far more important than simply knowing I have a journal-writing habit or that I like taking walks. The commonality among my husband's activities reveals that he is competitive and has an insatiable love for mastering new things. From working on a new piece of equipment to developing proper technique at a sport, to starting a business, or even renovating a space, he embraces experiences where change is constant. If I didn't understand that about him, I could easily be frustrated by the steady stream of new and different activities and events being introduced into our lives.

Jack, twelve years old, provides another good example. He spends evenings or lazy weekend afternoons doing everything from making and flying paper airplanes to building with Legos, taking a weekly pottery lesson, or teaching himself how to edit videos on a family computer. Some well-intentioned person might suggest to Jack that he be a pilot or an architect or maybe even a world-renowned potter when he grows up, but what is more important than trying to channel him to a specific career path of our choosing is noticing that given free time, Jack gravitates towards activities that allow him to use his hands.

Focusing on common characteristics among activities pushes us to think less about *what* specific hobbies we enjoy and more about *why* we enjoy these pursuits. This deeper-level approach encourages us to be expansive rather than restrictive in our thinking. By better understanding our preferences we can explore a myriad of other settings with those same qualities. For example, I might also enjoy knitting, swimming, photography, or graphic design as they, too, are all activities that allow me to be alone and have quiet. Twelve-year-old Jack benefits from realizing he likes using his hands because it can help him make decisions about everything from summer camp experiences to the volunteer service hours required for school. If Jack understands this connection between his hobbies and his likes or dislikes, he will have a lot of interesting and helpful information to use when settling on a major or future career. He can discern among theoretical liberal arts majors or a four-year degree in concentrations like filmmaking or graphic design. Or, he might use what he knows about himself to decide that trade school is the best fit for him.

It's important to note that two people can enjoy the same hobby, but for entirely different reasons. Take stamp collecting. I imagine what appeals to those who collect stamps might vary from person to person. One might love the sorting and categorizing of stamps based on years and other criteria. Another might enjoy the historical aspect, researching a stamp's origin and why it was commissioned. Still another might be drawn to the challenge of treasure hunting for rare stamps of great value, or appreciate the sheer artistry of commemorative stamps. Or what about the person who collects stamps because he loves socializing with like-minded people at the annual stamp collector's convention?

Whatever the activities or their commonalities, the goal of the Shine Method is to use hobbies to help people unearth important information about themselves that will help them become more confident decision makers.

Understanding why someone enjoys a hobby can go a long

way in unearthing important insights about a person's likes and dislikes. That information, when applied, can lead to more informed and confident decisions.

Take a minute to reflect on your hobbies. What qualities or characteristics do they have in common? When you think about some of them and consider them together, do any of them make you feel similarly? For instance, if you love both playing doubles tennis and group scrapbooking, is it the socializing you love, the sense of achievement you feel when it's over, or the aesthetics of both coordinated clothes and colored cardstock? What other experiences could you involve yourself with that have similar characteristics? What do your preferences in hobbies teach you about patterns in your thoughts, feelings, and behaviors? Is it calm, challenge, precision, or relationships that your hobbies allow you to pursue? How might you apply what you've learned about hobbies to your current job, volunteer position, or family situation?

I = Interests and Irritants

There are two categories we consider when talking about the letter "I" in the acronym "SHINE." We'll cover our interests, as well as our irritants; those things in life that irritate us and rile us up. Both provide us with clues about where we might make our greatest contributions in life.

Interests

Hobbies and interests might easily be mistaken for one another, so let's take a minute to clarify the difference. In an earlier example, we learned that Jack pursued hobbies that allowed him to use his hands—things such as working with paper airplanes and Legos, pottery, and videography. Those are hobbies; things he engaged with firsthand. Interests differ in that they might be less accessible and therefore experienced at somewhat of a distance; something we might read an article or watch a video about online, but not have a degree in, or have as part of our day-to-day jobs. An interest for Jack might be cinematography, or films directed by Quentin Taratino. Or he can read about cinematography and explore it, or study the greatest cinematographers of all time, but at twelve years old that could be the extent of his involvement. I love the world of advertising and the psychology behind ads, but neither is a part of my job or the hobbies I pursue in my free time. Mostly, my interest in these areas just means I instinctively notice advertisements of all kinds and enjoy thinking about what underlying principles from them I might apply to my own work in the future.

Interests are as varied and plentiful as the individuals who have them. Nature, astronomy, vintage cars, fashion, the Enneagram, leadership, architecture, politics—these are all things a person might be interested in, but otherwise have no formal training or expertise in. These aren't things we get paid to do, and our interaction with them is limited enough that we wouldn't put it in the "hobby" category.

> Interests are topics that pique our curiosity and when they come up, we are likely to sit up and pay attention.

Additional examples make the distinction even clearer. Someone might read as a hobby, and a glance at his bookshelf would reveal his interest is in Civil War history. My mother used to garden as a hobby, but one look inside her house and you would have known that art and design were underlying interests. My neighbor advocates for environmental issues, but it's his hobby of beekeeping that occupies his evenings and weekends. My dear friend makes a hobby out of connecting like-minded people over coffee, but driving many of those interactions is an underlying interest in local politics and issues of social justice.

Interests do not have to evolve into hobbies. Kim loves flipping through fashion catalogs for current trends, but other than it influencing her own wardrobe, she has no involvement with fashion. Matthew enjoys Greek mythology and voraciously reads any books he can get his hands on, but other than feeding his own curiosity and dressing up as Hercules one Halloween, the subject matter remains only an interest. Elaine is interested in art, but has never pursued painting or drawing as a hobby. Interests are merely topics around which we have curiosity.

When we view topics we are curious about as clues to our uniqueness, we can start to integrate our interests into the work we do and the contributions we make to the world. My interest in leadership and human development does not need to be separate from the work I do. In fact, the approach I bring to my work may be a result of my unique collection of interests. During my tenure working in higher education, I served as director of a department that used a lot of student volunteers to coordinate programs for new students entering the university. I was able to apply my interests in leadership and human development to developing a year-long internship in leadership. The program allowed students to have a rich experience working in my office and, while at the same time affording me the chance to grow in an area where I have a lot of interest. When our interests are allowed to mesh with other areas of our lives, our contributions will leave unique imprints.

It is fun to think about how Elaine's work, or feelings about work, might change if she could weave her love of art into her responsibilities as a senior sales director for a national magazine. Maybe she would follow up with clients on notecards featuring famous works of art or carefully curate a piece of art clients would receive as an annual holiday gift. Matthew the middle-schooler might go from doing only what he must in school to enthusiastically developing expertise in Greek mythology by completing assignments in all his disciplines—from math to science to Spanish and English—through a single lens he cares about. Furthermore, when Matthew's interests are fed, they stand to become hobbies, and hobbies when fed could become a future major or career path. And what about Kim? There are more than three million teachers in the United States and it is energizing to think about how different schools could look and feel if the teachers and staff who filled them were encouraged to incorporate their unique interests. As a math teacher, Kim could mobilize students to produce an annual fashion show, using basic math and budgeting skills to assemble their featured outfits. If she partnered with favorite local shops, she might even have the beginnings of a school fundraiser.

What topics are you interested in? List three to five. What opportunities do you have during the course of a week to feed or share your interests? What are some ways you could infuse your interests into activities you are already doing—whether at school or work, in a volunteer position or your home—that would feed your interests in a typical week?

Irritants

Aurora is an environmentalist, working hard to preserve marshlands in a community where commercial property development is a priority for many investors. Her interest in nature feeds her knowledge about the fragility of ecosystems which, in turn, fuels her fury about the impact new construction will have on local wildlife. Her irritation with developers launched an activist movement that is going strong more than forty years later, and is a perfect example of how sometimes knowing what we *don't* want can help us clarify what we *do* want.

In Aurora's case, knowing that she did not want bird nests displaced by buildings helped her clarify a contribution she could make to her community. People such as Martin Luther King, Jr., Marie Curie, Bill Gates, and Susan B. Anthony also provide insight into how our greatest irritants can, in fact, become the source of what might be our greatest contributions.

Martin Luther King, a local minister in Montgomery, Alabama, had for years been deeply disturbed by the segregation of black people in the southern United States. So when he was named to lead an organization fighting local bus segregation, he became the catalyst for peaceful protests in Montgomery, and then elsewhere, becoming a leader in the movement that eventually brought about passage of the Civil Rights Act and the Voting Rights Act in the 1960s. Marie Curie, the first woman to win a Nobel Prize and the only person to win a Nobel in two different sciences, combined her expertise and a problem she saw during World War I to develop the first mobile radiography units to aid physicians working on the battlefields of Europe. In the case of Bill Gates, after he had made his fortune building Microsoft, his inability to accept disparities in people's access to health care, among other things, prompted his greatest legacy—the Bill & Melinda Gates Foundation, which works to enhance health care, reduce poverty, and improve access to education and technology worldwide. Susan B. Anthony's discontent at women's lack of voting rights compelled her to serve as an organizer for the women's suffrage movement. In each of these cases, an irritant served as the impetus for someone creating a vision, then tapping into their talents to make it a reality.

Isn't this ultimately what community is all about—people coming together, bringing to bear what they have to offer, and creating a whole that is greater than the sum of our individual parts?

Using irritants to inspire change is a dynamic that can also motivate members of our own local communities. I look around at my own community and my mind turns immediately to the neighbor who started a Meals on Wheels program intended to fill needs of our senior citizens. Or I think about the certified dietician who works in a health food store because she sees the need to arm people with the information necessary to make healthy lifestyle choices. And then there is the entrepreneur who just couldn't accept there wasn't a better, faster way to get customers what they needed and, eleven years later, is using the company he started to fill a need in the healthcare industry. There are examples all around us of everyday people who were moved to action by a need or an injustice they saw in their corner of the world.

Creating space in schools and communities where people can think and talk about people who need help or problems that need attention is a great way to purposefully channel negativity into positive outcomes. Annually, House of Shine gets to participate in a year-long project assigned to students at a local school. Students are challenged to spend one year researching and developing, then implementing a project around a topic they care about. Our involvement is in offering a process that helps students come up with their topics. The project culminates in a community event where local stakeholders preview students' topics and provide additional resources, referrals, and helpful feedback.

LeaderShape® is an organization that puts on a six-day summer institute where college students envision a more caring and just world. Students imagine a change they would like to effect, then set about developing a blueprint for first steps they can implement when they return to campus.

Not all people are qualified to solve or interested in solving the same problems. True fulfillment comes when the contribution we make to the outside world matches our unique combination of interests and talents. If we all commit to sharing our shine with our communities, we'll experience multiple and diverse improvements to the world in which we live.

How about you? What ruffles your feathers and leaves you feeling irritable? Can you recall examples from your past when frustration might have fueled you to take action? What about right now? Is there an injustice, an inequity, or a something going on at home, at work, or in your friend group that needs resolution? Which of your talents and interests could you use to help resolve the irritant?

A Word about Pearls

The imagery of pearls is an interesting way to illustrate the value of acknowledging irritants, as opposed to ignoring or minimizing them. Loosely understood, the formation of a pearl begins with an irritant—in this case a tiny parasite or the proverbial grain of sand. The oyster tries defending itself against the irritant by encapsulating it with cells that then coat the irritant with a composite material. The process persists until, anywhere from 24 months to seven years later, a valuable gemstone is ready to be harvested.

The analogy of the pearl is helpful when talking to anyone from young students to corporate executives because it helps us illustrate a few key points:

1. From an irritant can come something valuable.

2. The irritant is encased and coated when we "react" to a problem we care about by bringing our talents and gifts to bear. Our innate talents are, in fact, our strongest resources and when we apply them to a particular problem, we stand to produce a gemstone.

3. Creating anything of value takes time. Like the oyster, we must stay with the process, believing that continued and repeated effort will yield the results we want.

N = *Needs*

"If I just had more time I would . . ." I remember uttering those words frequently in the last job I had as dean of students, before deciding to leave higher education and forge my own path. I would end the sentence with activities and actions such as:

- Read more
- Write more

- Bake more
- Be in better touch with my friends
- Exercise daily
- Have a perfectly organized home
- Update the pictures in my picture frames

Looking back, I realize now that this verbal wish list was just a safe way to articulate my unmet needs. I was proclaiming how—if I had had more time—I would have chosen to do things other than what I was then doing. The disconnect between how I was spending my time and how I wished I was spending my time revealed a gap between my thoughts and actions. If there is a disconnect between what a leader says is important to her and what she does, we would not consider her behavior principled. Conversely, when an outdoor clothing company such as Patagonia reinvests in the environment through the conservation organizations they support and the eco-friendly ways they do business, we tout them as having strong core values. The same is true for you and me: Learning how to keep our beliefs and actions aligned is important because it's the coherence between the two that allows us to live with integrity and experience an overall sense of peace.

> We develop core values over time and every day we make decisions that either support those values or challenge them.

You would be correct if, after you read my list, you commented that reading more, writing more, and baking more could not possibly be on my short list of core values. The activities I listed were simply symptoms of a bigger problem—that I was living out of alignment. The daily decisions I was making and the daily life I led did not include those things I believed I needed to be happy. My yearning for these activities was really my interest in reconnecting with core values that I felt slipping away.

- I wanted to read more because I value learning and expertise. Though my job was rigorous, it was filled with a lot of fruitless and mundane tasks.

- I wanted to write more because I value creativity. I got to do a certain amount of creative work in my position, but these isolated incidents always left me wishing for more.

- I wanted to bake more because I value generosity and gratitude. I pictured myself delivering beautifully packaged treats accompanied by thoughtfully written notes to all sorts of deserving people. But my intentions were far bigger than my reserve of energy at the end of a long workday.

- I wanted to be in better touch with my friends because I value friendship and loyalty. My evening commute was the best time to dial up a friend, but talking on the way home conflicted with another one of my needs—quiet time—so I never did this. As a result, I spoke less often with friends.

- I wanted to exercise more because I value health and discipline. Most weekday mornings I made it to the gym for an hour-long power workout, but the slower-paced walking and meditation sessions that I wanted, I never had time for.

- I wanted an organized home because I value order, but again, this couldn't compete with the demands of a rigid work schedule. Organized drawers and streamlined closets turned out to be an easy concession to make.

- I wanted updated pictures in my picture frames because I value aesthetics and attention to detail. Along with my closets and drawers, however, this activity went years without ever rising to the top of my list of priorities.

It would be easy to dismiss my short list of simple wants and needs as frivolous. After all, I had a good job that I generally enjoyed and which I was paid fairly well to do. That is exactly the point of my minor examples—these are things all of us can relate to, even if your list looks a little different. Why, when we go through the thoughtful work of understanding what we need to feel happy, would we then make concessions, turning our backs on these very things (especially when the things we need are relatively minor)? These seemingly small things, overlooked for a lifetime, can turn out to be big things. Family time, balance, travel; none of those needs is unreasonable, but when we dismiss them as being unrealistic or something we'll do more of when we retire, we run the risk of biding our time instead of enjoying the happiness we deserve right now.

Values help us realize that our lives are a series of choices. Every day we are called upon to make decisions, large and small, that either support the idea of the person we envision ourselves to be; or they contradict that idea. We alone are the ones who must eventually reconcile the decisions we make during our lifetime. We can do this all at once at the end of our lives, deciding in the short term to close our eyes and avoid, ignore, or dismiss the subtle cues that signal to us that we've gotten off-course. Or we can make minor adjustments along the way and in so doing enjoy a more satisfying journey. In the short run, the accountability and change required can feel scarier and harder than maintaining the status quo, but in the long run we are rewarded with greater fulfillment.

Scared is how I felt when I left my good and predictable life in higher education for an unknown future that I hoped would let me reprioritize some of my core values. My less structured workday meant the onus was now on me to organize my time so that I would be acting in closer accordance with what I knew would enhance my sense of fulfillment. If I didn't do this, I would have no one to blame but myself; but if I did persevere in making this change, I stood to have an even more rewarding life. And so I did. I focused on walking, baking with my boys, reading books about leadership and human development, making fun creations to give friends and other deserving people, and writing blog posts. I was happy.

Something interesting happened over time. The reading, writing, journaling, blogging, and creating led to more. More thoughts. More opportunities. More work. More demands on my days. And more structure. And then, eventually; less. Less reading, less writing, less journaling, less blogging, less creating; and then I was less happy. We are good at things we find fulfilling, and that often attracts other people and opportunities. Ultimately, the challenge we face in naming and claiming what makes us feel happy and fulfilled is only matched by the challenge of being in-tune enough to sense when we are falling out of balance. I am, in fact, in Florida right now, alone, writing this book. It's an overture toward once again reclaiming things I know I need to feel happy and fulfilled. The balancing act is one we must be prepared to calibrate and recalibrate for our entire lives.

Because of the infinite variations and combinations of what makes each of us happy, there can be no such thing as copying from a friend or acquiescing to the needs of your spouse or pushy boss. You can concede for a while, but eventually if your head and your heart are at all connected, one or the other will let you know the life you are living is not in alignment with what you need to feel happy and fulfilled.

Your turn. Ask yourself, "If I just had more time I would . . ." What items would you include on your list? Who would you have to talk to or what might you have to renegotiate in order to reprioritize what has fallen by the wayside? Can you look back and see where more, more, more has actually led to less, less, less? What could you do to bring things back into balance?

It's Everyone's Business to Be Happy

When I was in junior high and high school my father dropped me off at volleyball practice every morning. As part of the morning ritual, he would recite the same chant as I exited the car: "Claudia, Claudia, she's our man, if she can't do it, nobody can." That might seem funny in this day and age, but I heard it as a vote of confidence from someone who knew me best. That empowering message embedded itself in my psyche over the course of years and has paid dividends during my lifetime. Of course, I have come to realize how lucky I was to have a father who was both my literal and fig-urative cheerleader, and I understand not everyone is so fortunate. For you, maybe words of encouragement came from relatives, teachers, youth leaders, friends, or friends' parents. Or perhaps positive self-talk is the first real source of support you've received.

The other thing my father did during our morn-ing drive was plant seeds; nuggets of wisdom around topics he thought mattered. I will never forget the morning he said, "You know, Claudia, it's everybody's business to be happy." What he meant was that it's everyone's job to take responsibility for their own happiness. Our lives—like yours—were peppered with people who assigned responsibility for their happiness to everyone but themselves. Someone was unfair to them, they didn't have a job they liked, or they wished for more money, a better figure, or a spouse who was more ambitious. Whatever the reason, their lack of happiness and personal fulfillment was always someone else's doing.

Years later, this concept of knowing our needs is one of the most important elements of the Shine Method. People who shine are, above all else, happy and fulfilled, and achieving that state not only demands we know what brings us happiness and fulfillment, it also means we have the courage to ask for it; to advocate for ourselves in such a way we make it our own business to be happy.

I included needs as an aspect of self-awareness because I want people to feel they have permission to create individual expectations around things such as personal relationships, work environments, classrooms, and daily schedules. I say "permission" because sometimes these conversations can leave us feeling needy, pushy, or self-absorbed and our defensive walls go up as we try to guard against a growing sense of entitlement. The intent of talking about needs is not about entitlement, but empowerment. Knowing our needs is the foundation for holding ourselves accountable. This means that we are the architects of our own happiness and that if something is amiss, we will turn inward to determine what that problem is and how to fix it. This idea of holding ourselves accountable applies to the corporate executive unsure if he's suited for his job; the student evaluating his choices in friends, colleges, majors, or a career; single people discerning between dating partners; and even retirees planning for their future. Wherever people are making choices, room should be made for a discussion about needs.

E = Experiences

If you believe, as we do at House of Shine, that each of us is wired to make our own individual contribution to the world, it is reasonable to assume the mark we make is somehow influenced by where we have been, what we have seen, and who we have met along the way. My friend Amy is one good example.

At the time that I was writing this book, she was working on one of her own: a compilation of life lessons for college students based on her thirty years of listening to students' stories from a "Life Chair" that's been sitting in the corner of her office since she started working. Woven into the chair's fabric are stories filled with joy, sadness, despair, fear, vulnerability, hope, and everything in between. Amy's vantage point is special. Beloved by students, parents, faculty, staff, and alumni, she combines her credibility with her creativity and entrepreneurial spirit; Amy can produce a book that is as unique as she is.

It is possible to enjoy some of the same strengths, engage in some of the same hobbies, and even to share similar interests, irritants, and needs as other people you know. The chance, however, of having all these things in common with another person and also having identical life experiences is slim to none. This should instill in us a sense of both urgency and possibility.

> We can look to our left, look to our right, and never find another person wired exactly the way we are—we are truly set up to make a unique contribution.

No one else can offer what we can, in the way we can. Every person has a treasure trove of talents to be shared.

My friend Debbie was the daughter of a military man, meaning that her family moved a lot when she was a kid. Debbie is convinced that this is one of the reasons she can now as an adult so easily jump in and make friends wherever she and her husband—now in the military—decide to move. Both of my sisters took the train to New York City every day to attend the High School of Performing Arts. Today they both live in Manhattan, soaking up the experiences of living in the "city that never sleeps." It's a preference both agree was acquired during their teenage years. My friend Heather grew up in a large family that struggled financially, so she and her husband have a smaller family and two stable, professional positions. Another friend of mine grew up in a big family and loves reminiscing about all the great times she and her siblings had. Maintaining close family relationships is a core value and need of hers, so trips back home to Illinois happen every chance she gets. The same is true of you and me. When I was a teenager, I was a camp counselor, and this is where I got my first taste of leading others. The fact is, our life experiences influence how we think, feel, and behave.

It goes without saying not all experiences are created equal, yet when applying the Shine Method, even the worst of the worst experiences have a hand in shaping the contribution only we are meant to make. Having divorced parents might have meant being shuffled from one household to another on the weekends; though not ideal, that very experience might also explain why someone is so adaptable, resilient, independent, and resourceful. A stay-at-home mom might have started crafting cards because she felt isolated, but today that hobby has become a lucrative side hustle. A person who could have chosen any career path might have developed a serious interest in medicine because he was a sickly child or the child of a terminally ill parent. Perhaps someone you know became a teacher because she was bullied as a kid and wanted to foster an environment where young people felt cared for. These examples make clear how unpleasant experiences can become the source of our greatest attributes and, eventually, even our greatest contributions.

Though I was lucky enough to have had had a generally enviable childhood growing up, there were negative experiences that influenced me and helped shape choices I made along the way. In fourth grade, when I was finally diagnosed with dyslexia, my parents enrolled me in a parochial school where class sizes were smaller than the local public school and the chances were good that I might get more attention from my teachers. This change had nothing to do with religion because, although my mother grew up Catholic, my father was Jewish. (We celebrated Christian holidays, but more because they were festive and my mother was the

Chief Creator of Pomp and Circumstance in our house.) I knew very little about either religion, but I quickly learned how much I hated First Friday Mass. This was the day of the month when the Catholic students, one after another, weaved their way through the pews to the altar, so the priest could reward those in the "inner circle" with communion. As I wasn't Catholic, instead of fitting in, I stood (or in this case sat) out, while every other student in the school passed by me to collect their serving of approval from the priest.

Enduring the discomfort of all those First Friday Masses left indelible marks on my life. These marks have in turn influenced my strengths, hobbies, interests and irritants, and yes, even future experiences. I maintain that having to overcome my dyslexia to be a success at school gave me a drive and a work ethic that carried me straight through to getting my Ph.D. and, later, to starting up my own nonprofit. This experience probably also fueled my interest in education and human development (it most certainly created an additional layer of stress), as I sweated my way through four graduate-level statistics classes.

The parochial school experience also created some sore spots (irritants) for me. One example is the separateness I have always felt toward organized religion. I consider myself deeply spiritual, but formalized religions where some people are in and some people are out strike me as running counter to religion's intended purpose. For that reason, I've always protected myself by keeping a safe distance from organized religion. That experience of separateness also instilled in me a core value around inclusion, which had a residual impact on the positions I accepted and the ways I approached my workplaces ever after. From my RA position in college to the focus of my work as Dean of Students to the way we've embedded House of Shine programs into our local community, bringing people together is always a top priority for me.

Going through school with dyslexia and with my particular family background was not ideal: Yet, being singled out, and having my unique combination of strengths, interests and irritants, and needs, provided a backdrop to my life that looks different from anyone else's. And it is against this backdrop that I have been able to make a contribution in my corner of the world that is different from anyone else's.

The same is true for you. What have been some of your formative experiences in life—good ones and bad? Consider the first one that pops into your mind, and think through how it has subsequently influenced the ways you've behaved and decisions you have made.

A Composite Picture

Now that you have been introduced to all five letters of the word "shine," I hope you have greater appreciation for how you are wired to make contributions in the world that are different from those made by anyone else. By extension, maybe it also gives you greater appreciation for the people in your life—friends, family, or colleagues—who approach life differently than you do, but who nonetheless are also wired to make important contributions.

I, for one, know that absorbing these lessons has changed the way I parent my children. Rather than believing my job is to raise them for success as I define it, I now see my job as more like that of an archeologist. I spend time asking questions and making observations that will help my children unearth their own talents and gifts. I point out artifacts and traces of evidence that might help them spot patterns in the ways they think, feel, and behave. By helping my boys cultivate strong self-awareness, I am arming them with an inner compass they can carry with them for the rest of their lives. No matter where they go or what life throws at them, they will be secure in who they are and how they can use what they know to craft a fulfilling life.

Answering the *Pick Up the Phone* questions at the end of each of the "S-H-I-N-E" sections is a great first step toward becoming more self-aware. Deciding to share the questions with friends, family members, classmates, and colleagues can open an even bigger door to meaningful conversations about the roles each of us can play in making our corner of the world better. What we can hope for (and work towards) is that eventually we can replace some of the apathy and indifference we encounter daily with engaged communities where contribution is part of the ethos.

In the next chapter we will explore how with the privilege of natural-born talents and strengths comes the responsibility of doing something with them.

CHAPTER 3

Do

"Do" is the second part of the Shine Method. It is where we transition from discovering what engages and delights us to reflecting on what we've learned about ourselves. This section contains actionable steps to further develop and refine the talents and gifts that we have unearthed.

Congratulations, You Now Have a Gym Membership

As someone who has played sports and been committed to an exercise regimen for most of my life, I like to use fitness analogies when talking about the responsibility we have to our

Shine—the unique combination of talents and gifts given to us at birth that shape who we are. Imagine that purchasing this book was like purchasing a membership to a local gym. All the membership card really does is give you permission to cross the threshold into the building and use the equipment. It says nothing about your level of fitness or how much you know about using the equipment. Similarly, buying this book and holding it in your hands is just possessing access to the information. It says nothing about how bright you shine or how readily you will apply the concepts.

To actually Shine—to know who you are and why this matters—you must roll up your sleeves, get inside the pages of this book, and flex your Shine Muscles. That is to say, you must commit to the regular practice of thinking and behaving like someone who considers herself an elite athlete of life.

You wish the next ten pages or so were filled with your personalized workout plan, don't you? That would be easy: *Do x, y, and z and be guaranteed abs of steel and the definitive answer to your purpose in life!* If only it was that simple. I can exercise next to the same woman in a barbell class every morning and still not have her perfectly sculpted calves. Our shapes and genetics are different, our metabolisms are different, and our eating habits are probably different. Similarly, as I spent the first half of this book trying to convince you, our gifts and talents, and everything else that makes up our unique individual

Shine, are different, so applying a rote formula will take you only so far. You need to engage with your unique self, and do it consistently.

The pages of this book are an invitation to come to the gym and to receive an orientation for how each piece of equipment works. After that, the choice is yours as to how committed you will be; whether you will become a morning regular or whether you will start out strong and let your workouts peter out after the first few weeks. We certainly hope you will keep coming back.

Shine Muscles

Depending on whether you're counting only skeletal muscles (the muscles that move our bodies) or all muscles (such as the heart), there are anywhere from 650 to 800 muscles in the human body. While most of us can't name more than a few of them, we count on our muscles working together with the rest of our anatomy to perform everyday tasks such as walking, climbing, and digesting food. Of our ten or so muscle groups, most of us visit the gym hoping to flex about six to eight of them. We want well-defined biceps and triceps; quads, hamstrings, and calves we are proud of; strong abdominal and back muscles for stabilizing; and if we're really going for broke a gluteus maximus that fits nicely into our favorite pair of jeans. When those six to eight muscle groups are working well, our bodies feel strong and seem to move almost effortlessly.

The same is true of our Shine Muscles; when they are strong we seem to move through life with less effort. You might imagine Shine Muscles, like regular muscles, are also made up of hundreds or even thousands of muscle fibers. Only in this case, the fibers represent countless patterns in the way you think, feel, and behave. When those patterns are grouped together, they create a muscle that helps you move through life. If the muscle is weak, the decisions we make do not support the life we envision for ourselves. If the muscle is well-defined, the decisions we make feel strong.

At House of Shine, our Shine Muscles come from exercising the ten Shine Principles. We settled on these ten after years of observing and interviewing people who stood out in their communities, as these were the characteristics most often represented. They work in combination and not all of them are firing at one time. That is to say, we might exhibit one or two of these principles at a time, while others seem to be dormant. Imagine it as being like climbing a flight of stairs, where your leg muscles are working hard and your triceps are in a more relaxed state. And, of course, some days it's as though we barely budge from the couch, which is to say those days when our thoughts and actions are not those of someone who shines:

We're in a bad mood, feeling impatient, or making decisions we aren't proud of.

> None of us shines all the time, but the goal is to "get to the gym" more days than you don't.

The Shine Principles work in combination but, like the muscles in our bodies, not all of them fire at the same time. Understanding that eliminates any expectation people might have that to shine (or be fit), we must behave a certain way (or exercise) all day every day.

Below is a brief description of the ten Shine Principles. First, let's go through each one; then we'll look at strategies for putting them to work in your life.

Be Present

Shining requires us to stop multitasking and looking past the present moment for something better around the corner. It means making informed decisions about how and with whom we spend time and then trusting that focused efforts in the here and now will result in feeling fulfilled and satisfied.

Nothing productive comes from you wishing you were somewhere else or doing something different.

As I am writing this paragraph, members of my family are on a boat in the bay outside my window. I chose to stay back because on this particular afternoon writing this book is more important than having fun in the sun. I could pine over missing out on family time or resent the sacrifice I am making, but I'd already made my choice. Now I am here at my desk, and my job is to fully embrace the time alone, so I can get from it the full benefit of a quiet house. When we are present, we give ourselves over to whatever it is we are doing and accept the fullness of that moment. If, during the evening or weekend, we are spending time with our children, we resist the urge to think about the more pressing tasks we could be doing. When we sit down to a meal with others, we declare it a phone-free zone and get drawn into meaningful conversations rather than distractions from our media notifications. Preoccupation with the past and future undermines the potential embedded in life's present moments.

Create

People who shine push boundaries. They are masters of their trade and that mastery allows them to see opportunities for improvement. They are not afraid to create.

People who shine plow through the fear and uncertainty of taking risks, because they are excited by the idea of breaking ground on something new.

Creators appear in every industry, from the artist who experiments with a new medium to the surgeon who develops a new medical procedure. She could be an architect breaking ground on an awe-inspiring skyscraper or a barista developing a new recipe. He could be a teacher training others on lab equipment for teaching STEM or an engineer introducing the "Best New Consumer Product of the Year." Or in your neighborhood, he could be the Little League coach who shows up to practice with a new set of drills for his team or the twelve-year-old who writes a proposal to her principal about a better way to manage the car line outside the school. Creators are catalysts for improvement.

Use Your Strengths

We've already spent a good deal of time talking about strengths. People who shine realize that each of us possesses a unique combination of strengths and when we feed these qualities with knowledge and skills, we develop talents we can then use to make a significant contribution in the world. Shining means not only discovering what your talents are, but also unleashing them in your world. Living from your strengths also means knowing yourself—the good, the bad, and the ugly. It means choosing daily to focus on your attributes, deciding how to use them, and spending less time thinking about how to best overcome your deficits. Time is a limited resource; time spent compensating or hiding weaknesses is time not spent sharing the very quality that makes you shine.

Keep Perspective

People who shine are able to maintain their sense of context. They accept that their thoughts and actions will not always feel like those of someone who shines, but they manage those negative feelings by taking action around activities they believe will improve their outlook.

People who shine appreciate what they have and empathize with others' struggles.

Without perspective we lose sight of our lives in relation to the rest of our community, city, state, and country. We can indulge ourselves in believing our problems are so big we can't possibly spare the energy needed to help another person. Lacking perspective on the real scale of our concerns, we can wallow in our own misery until it becomes an excuse for not helping. Connecting to the bigger picture is part of what makes us shine.

Realize the Impact of Little Things

Shining means holding yourself accountable for being as good at the little stuff as you are at the big stuff. A small candle flickering over a romantic table for two can create a joyous moment every bit as meaningful as floodlights illuminating a football stadium during a championship game. When you shine, you treat small opportunities with as much importance as the big ones. It means your presentation for ten people warrants every bit as much preparation as the keynote address for hundreds. It means accepting that fifteen minutes spent reading a book to your child nightly might actually mean more than a week at Disneyland. Shining means not minimizing the importance of small gestures, and not thinking we can make up for them with periodic grand gestures. Small gestures can be more inconvenient, disrupting already overcommitted schedules. But in the end those small gestures can have an impact much larger than our more controlled, episodic gestures of generosity.

Bring Out the Best in Others

If you accept that you have a unique set of talents and gifts to share with the world, you must also accept that the same is true of everyone around you. Everyone has something to offer and everyone feels better when their talents are used and acknowledged.

> Shining means that while you are busy discovering your unique contribution to the world, you are also helping others discover theirs.

There is a lot of world to shine in: 104 million square miles of habitable Earth. Helping someone else shine does not mean you shine any less. In fact, the opposite is true. Those who shine brightest are those who help others connect with their own Shine.

Reject Mediocrity

People who shine don't just check boxes or look for how to squeak by doing as little as possible. Instead, people who shine take pride in their work and therefore give their best effort in what they choose to do. Students who shine attend classes and do readings because they know the work they do today will better prepare them for passionate careers tomorrow. Hourly employees who shine don't show up at work prepared to bide time until their shift is over; they arrive at work looking for ways to add value. Shining results from cultivating the kind of confidence that only comes from knowing that you are giving your personal best.

Be Relentlessly Passionate

People who shine are relentless; fixated on their passions, they work tirelessly to reach their goals. If the goal of someone who shines is to maintain balance by exercising daily, then he will make time for exercise—no excuses. This energy to persist comes from a deep sense of purpose. You can see it in the English teacher who will not rest until his students can read and write, and have cultivated an appreciation for good literature. It's also discernible in the social entrepreneur who fights to combine business savvy with philanthropy, because she is convinced that success in one area will breed success in the other. You will find among people who shine a sense of purpose. Though they often receive accolades and recognition from others, that recognition is not what motivates them: People who shine do what they love because they cannot imagine an alternative. So committed are they to their cause, to their passion, that their real satisfaction comes from knowing their contribution makes a difference. Their drive to shine comes from within.

Be Accountable

For every compelling reason for us to live a full, rich life, there are an equal number of reasons to cut corners, overlook, justify, and rationalize. People who shine understand that choosing to shine is a habit, like exercising, managing money, or becoming more patient. That is why people who shine *practice* shining. They catch themselves in the midst of cutting a corner, acknowledge it, and then in a disciplined way switch gears. People who shine not only hold themselves accountable, they also are able to adhere to their chosen goals.

Spread Shine

People who shine know that by sprinkling Shine around in their corner of the world, sparks are created that will ignite others. They know that the ten minutes spent recognizing the hardworking handyman or the compassionate day care provider reinforces someone's Shine. They know that an unexpected message written in sidewalk chalk or an anonymous note left on a windshield can cast a light far enough and wide enough to illuminate an entire neighborhood. Armed with this information, people who shine build time into their week for recognizing the goodness of others' contributions. Shining is a highly contagious attitude that is most easily transmitted through the celebration of people and events.

How fit are your Shine Muscles? Do some need more strengthening than others? Do you see how regularly flexing any one of those ten muscles would contribute to your overall health and wellness? Consider drawing a star next to those muscles you consider to be in good shape, and a circle beside the Shine Muscles you think could stand being stretched or flexed more often.

Shine Workouts

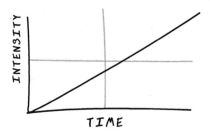

If the ten Shine Principles are the Shine Muscles we are most actively trying to engage, we'll now focus on how we can go about exercising them. To start, let's return to the gym/work-out analogy. So, let's imagine you are standing in the center of a gym with a good 360-degree view of everything going on around you. You notice that people are exercising for different lengths of time and with different levels of intensity. The person to your left, Person 1, is doing as little as possible. He showed up, and is maybe even wearing athletic clothing, but the sole extent of his effort is to stand and listen to someone else tell him what he could do to strengthen his leg muscles. At the end of thirty minutes, after only a few repetitions he's back out the door. Person 2 is walking on the treadmill. Though her speed isn't especially ambitious, you do recall having seen her here at the gym working out six days a week. Person 3 isn't as much of a regular as the woman on the treadmill, but you recall that you've noticed that his occasional thirty-minute power workouts require quite a bit of energy. Then there is Person 4: She has built the gym into her regular morning routine, showing up five out of seven days a week, for two hours at a time. You've seen her high-intensity workout as she goes from machine to machine, lifting free weights in between, and engaging each of her muscle groups.

The level of fitness each of these four people enjoys is correlated to the frequency and amount of physical and psychological energy they exert during their workouts. The same is true of people's commitment to Shine.

The success we experience correlates with the frequency and intensity of effort we exert doing what it takes to live out the ten Shine Principles.

It's worth noting that there are days in which all I do at my local gym is "place-hold." This is a term I use to describe my workouts when I wake up dreading the idea of going to the gym. My body is tired, my mind is distracted, and the only thing getting me there is an awareness of how much worse I would feel if I didn't go at all. In those instances, I place-hold; giving myself permission to do as little as I want, just so long as I cross the threshold. It works because, to paraphrase Newton's first law of motion: What's in motion stays in motion. Placeholding buys me just enough time to have my internal level of motivation catch back up with the loftier vision I have for myself.

Of course, you don't need a gym membership to be fit. Similarly, there is not a single prescribed way to exercise your Shine Muscles. The key is to make a daily decision you will show up to do something—anything—that gets you closer to living the life you envision for yourself. The following pages offer suggestions about how you might exercise your Shine Muscles, based on how much time and intensity you want to bring to your "workouts."

Short, Low-Intensity Workout

SHINE WORKOUT #1
SHORT, LOW-INTESITY

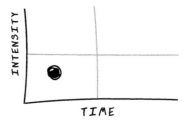

In life I would categorize myself as a late adopter. I am usually one of the last people to jump on board with a new trend or fad that others have, months earlier, incorporated into their lives. I find that dipping my toe in the water—rather than jumping in hook, line, and sinker—allows me to experience change gradually, while I can observe its effects and make adjustments. These workouts do that. They allow you to exert a little bit of energy, over a short period of time, so you can get a sense of what it feels like to integrate the Shine philosophy into your life for the long term. Here are some simple ideas to get you moving:

- Schedule a coffee date with a friend.
- Read a book.
- Listen to a podcast.

- Take a personality test, such as CliftonStrengths, DiSC, or Enneagram.
- Send a thank-you note.
- Volunteer one Saturday.
- Attend a Meetup group.
- Pay someone a compliment.

Like a walk around the block, these short, low-intensity workouts will get you moving in the right direction. The rush of satisfaction they provide will motivate you to seek more.

Long, Low-Intensity Workout

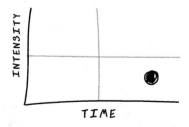

Experiences in this category often turn into valued rituals or traditions, because they generally span a longer period of time than those in the first category. They require only a moderate amount of physical and psychological energy, but the real work is committing to do them over a long period of time. They aren't one-and-done types of experiences. In fact, they are most impactful when we commit to them for a period of a year or more. I find this type of "workout for the soul" especially effective for the busy lifestyles so many of us manage, because rather than making large outlays of time or energy, we usually find smaller bits of time to commit over the long haul. Essentially, this is the same commitment many of us make when we agree to a thirty-year mortgage, paying only small amounts monthly.

Some examples of this workout include:

- Attend church or another spiritual gathering weekly.
- Join a book club.
- Journal.
- Take a thirty-minute walk outside three to five days a week.
- Contribute to your savings account monthly.
- Introduce a family ritual into your mealtime.
- Meditate once every day.
- Develop a new hobby.
- Learn a new language or musical instrument.
- Cultivate a new friendship.
- Participate in "DO 52" every week for a year.

Each of these suggestions provides opportunities to gently push ourselves beyond our comfort zone, but to do it in such a way that the experience is not all-consuming or exhausting.

DO52™: A Weekly Phone Call Between Your Head and Your Heart

As the creator of the Shine Method, I feel an additional imperative to be a good steward of its core principles and tenets—to walk the talk. On one occasion many summers ago, I could feel the growing number of deadlines and deliverables crowding out the time and space I needed to be creative. Yet I was already very clear on the connection between my happiness and my need for creative expression. Heading out of town for an extended vacation, I decided I would bring with me twenty-six randomly selected verbs (using a random word generator), one beginning with each letter of the alphabet.

On this vacation, each morning when I awoke I drew one of the verbs, then invited it into my day, imagining how I might use it to rejuvenate myself or to influence a decision I made or a creative endeavor I undertook. Each randomly selected verb was more fun than the next, as I moved from "leap" to "eliminate" to "decorate," "hug," "illustrate," "zoom," and twenty others. For example, the verb "eliminate" challenged me to think about how my habit of defaulting to conversations about how busy I was exacerbated my feelings of freneticism. That day I decided to *eliminate* "I'm so busy" from my vernacular. The verb "zoom" was a little tougher. I didn't think it would be smart to *zoom* in my car, so instead, while driving down Highway 1, I spotted a roadside banner advertising Zumba classes. I didn't know anything about Zumba, but I like to exercise, so I spontaneously pulled over and went inside to inquire when the next class would be. It started within minutes, and I was wearing athletic attire, so I decided this was the universe's way of approving my slight adaptation of "zoom." As it turned out, my hips don't move and shake the way they do for Zumba enthusiasts, but as I slithered out of class I reveled in the satisfaction of experiencing a new adventure.

When I returned home, feeling refreshed and completely reconnected to my creative side. I couldn't help but think, if this simple tool was so useful to me, it could also be useful to others. The idea of a verb-a-day was a little daunting, so I reworked the concept and instead imagined one verb a week for an entire year, and called it "DO52."

Today, we offer this product at House of Shine. We describe it as a weekly conversation between your head and your heart—you can use the annually curated verbs as fodder for your weekly discussions between the two. It underscores the fact that each of us already knows what it is we need to shine, but that the din of everyday life is so loud we can't always hear what's happening on the inside. Rarely do any two people use the same verb in similar ways, because each individual needs something different to feel like we are living our best life. Consider shaking things up in your life, your office, your classroom, or at your dinner table by getting a set of your own and participating in this weekly ritual. It will help you crystallize, and advocate for, your needs.

Short, High-Intensity Workout

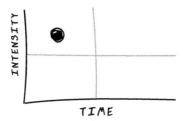

If you've ever been on a roller coaster you know the rush that can come from daring yourself to do something outside your comfort zone. These experiences bring a release of endorphins that temporarily leaves you feeling strong, and proud of what you've accomplished. Tackling the types of experiences included in this category involves something similar. None of them take long to do, but each of them requires a real commitment of effort, both physically and psychologically.

Examples include:

- Attend a weekend retreat with a local group.
- Participate in a self-help workshop.
- Check an item off your bucket list.
- Travel to a new place.
- Compete in an athletic event.

- Volunteer for a brief local campaign or to support a one-day event.
- Have a hard conversation.
- Tackle something that scares you.
- Conduct a conscious act of kindness.
- Take the "Be-Do-Share Challenge" outlined in the following section.

The burst of energy we exert on activities in this category (or quadrant) result in feelings similar to a runner's high. When an experience like this ends, you likely will begin to anticipate another opportunity to feel this way again.

Take the Be-Do-Share Challenge

As noted earlier, living a happy and fulfilled life is a daily decision we must make. It's a series of small disciplines, combined with intermittent larger acts of courage. The small disciplines are little decisions such as waking up thirty minutes early to fit in time for exercise, meeting weekly with an accountability partner who supports your goal of finishing a project, or trimming monthly expenses to save for an international trip you've dreamed of taking. Intermittent acts of courage happen less frequently, but they are bigger, and when we embrace them we create pathways for meaningful personal growth. Acts of courage can include stretching yourself to accept a job for which you do not feel fully qualified, purchasing a home for the first time instead of renting, or leaving a longstanding relationship that is unhealthy.

Our Be-Do-Share Challenge presents people with practical opportunities for experimenting with our Shine Principles. It's intended to move our ideas off the pages of this book and into the consciousness of your everyday life. Commit to taking the Be-Do-Share Challenge and you'll be on your way to shining brighter.

Be: Be curious. Be observant. Be a Shineologist. Decide you are going to use a journal to begin recording data about yourself. To get started, use the first few pages to write down these five things:

1. The headline from today's news. Also include a sentence or two discussing your opinion on the subject.

2. A business card from someone you recently met or a place you recently visited. What's your connection to the person or location?

3. Trace one of your hands, and in each of the five fingers add something you're proud to have completed.

4. A quote that inspires you.

5. A receipt, signature, or image that helps explain your morning routine.

Do: Do something today. Do something specific. Do something outside the ordinary. Take action this week on at least one of the ideas I have shared in this book. You might consider: setting up a meeting with someone you thought about while reading this book; discussing a chapter of this book at your dinner table tonight; or tucking yourself away in a coffee shop and answering the questions posed in each of the "Pick Up the Phone" sections.

Share: Share your talents. Share your interests. Share your best ideas. Brighten your corner of the world by committing to share your talents with someone in your community. If you love to bake, surprise someone with a batch of cookies. If you love dogs, make a donation to or volunteer at your local animal shelter. If you love ideas, share the best one you've got with us about how together we can power the planet with Shine. www.houseofshine.com

Long, High-Intensity Workout

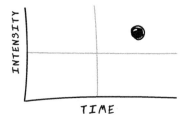

SHINE WORKOUT #4
SHORT, LOW-INTESITY

In athletics, this category of activity would be equivalent to running (and training for) a marathon. Participating successfully in these activities requires the largest commitment of time and energy. And the energy needed is not just physical: These activities also require quite a bit of psychological energy by way of self-reflection, combating our inner critic, overcoming fears, and potentially facing the disappointment of failure. Experiences in this quadrant have the potential to be some of the most rewarding and transformational, simply because we need to invest so much of ourselves in participating. Actions you could take in this category might include:

- Join a forum or other accountability group.
- Commit to a bible or other spiritual study group.
- Attend therapy.

- Serve as a mentor.
- Start a local club or organization.
- Register and then train for a future athletic competition.
- Chair an annual event for a local charity.
- Write a book or start a weekly blog or newsletter.

Experiences in this category are most likely to help us see ourselves in a whole new light and change our future behaviors. The sheer outlay of effort, combined with sustained commitment of time, redefines what we accept as the outer limits of our potential.

Replicability

A word about the importance of replicability. The reason "Do" is the second leg of the Shine Method is because doing—building, refining, and strengthening our Shine Muscles—is the only way to increase the likelihood of replicating our successes. It is through repeat successes that we find fulfillment and confidence.

We all want to believe we were born with a unique combination of talents and gifts. And we were. But most of us are also haunted by the fear we will be found out as an impostor—that the success we had was a one-time wonder, or that it's only a matter of time before our jig is up and people realize we aren't as good as they thought we were. In the early days of discovering and using our strengths this makes sense, because we haven't yet strung together enough successes to know what it is we are doing that works. For example, when I had just started developing and delivering workshops, I couldn't easily explain why I was able to capture the attention of my audience and then keep them engaged. Only after doing it again and again was I able to see how my combined use of storytelling, photographs, interactive handouts, and the element of surprise made me consistently successful. The key to developing that confidence is time and attention.

We must hone our craft and refine our innate talents and skills because having these things does not entitle us to them. When we are young most of us have pearly white smiles, but if we don't take care of the teeth we were given, our beautiful smiles go away. The same is true with our skin. Many teenagers sunbathe, slathering on suntan lotion and never imagining their skin will ever look anything but clear and taut. If we take our skin for granted, not tending to it with hats, sunglasses, and sunscreen, as we age its condition will worsen.

Our strengths operate in the same way. We have been given a gift—the gift of innate talents. If we use them, build them, and flex them and we can enjoy the kind of confidence that comes from knowing our successes are built upon a solid foundation; that they are not flukes or a series of coincidences.

> If we take our talents for granted and don't feed them, honor them, or encourage them, eventually they will do what muscles do when they are underutilized: They will atrophy.

Belief that we can repeat our successes builds confidence, and self-confidence is foundational to a person's willingness to engage again. Watch a student raise his hand to ask a question in the classroom and you will see exactly what I mean. When the student's question is met with curiosity and appreciation, the student becomes more confident that he is asking good questions, and he will likely do it again. But if the student is made to feel as though he interrupted class to ask something he should already know, insecurities will set in and his inclination to do it again likely will diminish. When the contribution you make is met with a positive response, you are affirmed, and since affirmations feel good, you have incentive to do it again. The more you repeat the behavior, whether it be contributing in the classroom, cooking dinner, facilitating a meeting, or problem solving, the better you get

STRENGTHENING SHINE MUSCLES:
CONTRIBUTION BREEDS CONFIDENCE

CONTRIBUTE

AFFIRMATION

STRENGTHEN
SHINE MUSCLE

CONTRIBUTE
AGAIN

GAIN CONFIDENCE

at it. The better you get at it, the more confident you become, and the more confident you become, the more willing you are to share that talent again and again. This notion of replicability applies to students in our classrooms, employees in our offices, or volunteers in our organizations—when you feel confident, you are more likely to engage and share your talents with the world.

CHAPTER 4

Share

Share, the third part of the Shine Method, is how we answer the question, "To what end?" Why does it matter if we understand how our strengths, hobbies, interests and irritants, needs, and experiences enable us to contribute in ways that are different from everyone else? And why should we go to the additional effort of refining innate talents and skills to the point where we can replicate successes again and again? This section seeks to answer those questions by showing the joy and fulfillment people experience when using their Shine to improve the world around them.

A Case for Sharing

**CYCLE OF SHARING
YOUR SHINE**

SHARE
SHINE

FEEL
HAPPY

UPLIFT
OTHERS

Weeks ago, a dear friend of mine mailed me a card or a care package every day for seven straight days. It was thoughtful, yes, but what made this gesture even more remarkable is that my friend was slogging her way through what was arguably one of the most difficult times in her life. Her marriage had dissolved after twenty years; health concerns had resurfaced; she had recently buried her mother; and her busy schedule was made busier when circumstances required her to step in and take care of her grandchild. Why then did Lori, in the midst of all that, shower me—who was doing fine—with snail mail?

She did it because Lori, and the interminable light within her, understands the healing properties associated with giving. She understands that when bad things happen it is easy to lose perspective and send yourself into a downward spiral. By extension, Lori also realizes the most surefire way of combating these feelings of hopelessness is to be generous towards others. Her outward focus allows Lori to expand her sphere, focusing less on the negativity immediately surrounding her and more on connecting herself to a larger, more compassionate universe.

I am a practical New Yorker type; a meat-and-potatoes, tell-it-like-it-is kind of girl, so discussions of "compassion" and the "universe" are not something that would have seemed likely for me five years ago. But my own experiences with House of Shine have made a compelling case for how sharing what we have—whether time, energy, or money—creates both abundance and happiness.

House of Shine started as a blog with me sharing one creative idea per day, so I suppose you could say I was sharing from the beginning. To be clear, at this particular time I was blogging because I was mad. I had left a career that I loved, in a town I'd fallen in love with, all because my husband's job required us to move. During the first year of that transition, blogging was the one thing I did that made me feel good about myself and kept me from wanting to fall into deep sadness about what had happened to the life I loved. Laundry didn't bring happiness, and neither did sorting mail, changing diapers, and wiping drool from Jack's face. Only the few hours each day that I got to be creative and write a blog post brought me fulfillment and a sense of accomplishment.

Yet the blog posts I was writing weren't just for me—they were intended to be read by others. And eventually the ideas I shared were all creative ways to recognize and thank others. I ended up creating a virtual platform where every day I was able to give to others by way of either content or accolades. This virtual platform even led to literal giving. I ran contests, mailed prizes, allowed visitors to earn patches, and even hosted an annual awards night for loyal readers.

With every idea and every item that I gave away, more energy was generated by me and my reader community. And the energy propelled me to do more. And the more I shared my ideas about recognizing people who shine and used those ideas to recognize people in my own community, the more House of Shine grew. And I loved the growth, because leading this community was where my talents and interests lay, and sharing my talents with other people made me feel happy. Therein lies the virtuous cycle between sharing and happiness. Look into the eyes of a baby to experience this phenomenon in its simplest form: When you smile at a baby and the baby smiles back at you, you cannot help but return an even bigger smile. The same is true of sharing our talents. We share these talents because it feels good and people respond favorably, so we cannot help but want to give more; giving more makes us feel good.

One Step Further: What Do We Share?

Asking ourselves questions about what we share is an important piece of the Shine Method. Conceivably we can share all kinds of things, but for it to make the greatest impact, what you share has to fit *you*. Setting up a blog to share tips on writing code, purchasing wine, or fixing cars would not have worked for me. That is to say, the insights I shared would not have been good, readers wouldn't have followed along, the community would not have grown, and my sharing would not have led to even more sharing. Pursuing any one of those topics would have led to a dead end because these topics were not things for which I had a talent or significant interest. This book began with an exploration of strengths, hobbies, interests and irritants, needs, and experiences because self-awareness is foundational to deciding what and how you will share with the world around you.

Talent, Interest, and Need

The third part of the Shine Method requires you to use what you learned about yourself in the "Be" and "Do" chapters. This information will help you answer three simple questions:

1. What are my *talents?*
2. What are my *interests?*
3. What *need* do I see in the world around me?

What Are My Talents?

The question about talents sends you back to Chapter 2, to the Shine Method where you explored your strengths, hobbies, interests and irritants, needs, and experiences. The talents you possess are embedded in your responses within each of those categories. When we reflect on the words or phrases we jotted down in each of those sections, chances are some common themes will emerge. It might be that woven through your answers is a thread of risk-taking, problem-solving, building relationships, or serving others. It keeps showing up because we naturally gravitate toward using our talents and strengths.

An audit of my Shine reveals recurring themes in areas such as: generating creative ideas, communicating, leading, teaching, planning and organizing. Whether they were expressed in the programs I planned as an RA or many years later as a blogger, my talents cluster around a relatively small group of attributes.

My thoughtful friend Lori, who I've known for over thirty years, has talents for building relationships, being a good listener, adapting to change, and connecting like-minded people.

My husband, the entrepreneur, has talents that include decisiveness, strategic-mindedness, an ability to separate the important from the urgent, and a genuine interest in building relationships.

What about you? When you connect the dots from your past successes and reflect on the answers to the "Pick Up the Phone" questions posed in Chapter 2, what are the talents you are most proud of?

What Are My Interests?

Again, an audit of your Shine will provide deeper insight into what subject matters interest you most. Of course, a good place to start is with the letter "I"—the exploration of your literal interests.

When I think about my mother, who was also very creative, I realize her interests were vastly different from mine. She enjoyed exploring creative endeavors such as the artistry of lace making, book-binding, and beading, and applying the principles of feng shui to the rooms in her house.

My colleague, Katie, is interested in traveling, journaling, leadership, the Enneagram, sports, and being outdoors.

And, at fifteen, my son Matthew is interested in Greek mythology, politics, playing tennis, reading, photography, and collecting hooded sweatshirts.

Interests, whether they come in the form of topics you would like to explore or irritants you would like to understand better, instill in us feelings of curiosity. It makes sense to factor curiosities into whatever contributions we share, because the contributions we make will require time and effort and when we are interested in what we are doing, we are more motivated to persist.

What conclusions can you draw when scanning your home for evidence of what you find interesting? Are there collections of books, sporting equipment, or cooking utensils? Do the apps on your phone or the podcasts you follow reveal interesting insights about topics you enjoy exploring? And what about the absence of artifacts? What might we learn about your interests by virtue of items that are nowhere to be found in your home? A lack of processed food in your kitchen, for example, might reveal an interest in wellness and nutrition.

The problem is not are there enough problems to go around; the world is full of them. Your only challenge is picking one.

What Needs Do I See in the World Around Me?

This can seem like a lofty question, one given weight by large-scale global problems such as crises involving the environment, hunger, and underserved populations. And these are important, but needs exist everywhere. Feel free to make note of needs you see in groups as small as your family or classrooms or as big as your state, country, or the whole world, and everything in between.

Another good place to begin thinking about needs is by doing an audit of the irritants you listed earlier. Chances are some of the needs you see in the world around you are the result of being "irritated" by perceived gaps or voids.

I am a good example. I look around and I see a void in quality time between so many parents and their kids. I notice families huddled around restaurant tables together, but preoccupied by their own handheld devices. Or, I notice preschoolers in car seats watching TV shows while being driven around town, as opposed to daydreaming or talking to whoever is driving. I see a void in the amount of time young people spend in self-reflection and a gap in schools' responses to facilitating experiences that foster reflection and self-awareness.

I've become acquainted with a young woman who sees a real gap in how educated people are about genetically modified foods (GMOs) and a lack of local eateries that are committed to providing non-GMO menu items.

I have a dear friend who is a member of her local Rotary Club. She sees an achievement gap between kids who have access to computers at home and those who don't, and she sees a void in services to help close that gap.

The list of gaps or voids in any given community is so long, the problem will never be whether there are enough needs to go around for every person who wants to contribute. Instead, the bigger question will always be how do community members choose the need they would like to help fill?

Pay attention to what's going on nationally, regionally, locally—wherever you want to make an impact. Read the headlines, listen to what folks are saying at the grocery store or coffee shop, or what's coming up at the local school board meetings. At House of Shine, we say, "Emotion is data." Notice what's evoking emotion around you and it will provide clues as to where help is needed.

Points of Intersection

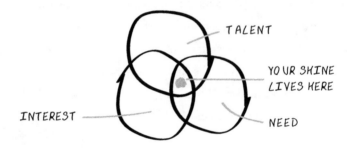

According to the Shine Method, the answer to which gaps in a community you are most equipped to fill lies in finding your Point of Intersection (POI). This final step in the Shine Method synthesizes what you have learned about yourself up to this point and helps you find a POI that excites you.

The beauty of using the POI is that:

- It works in any environment, such as families, schools, athletic teams, and corporations.
- It can be adjusted to fit the experience and skill level of whoever is using it.

- It empowers any person to tackle a problem they feel passionately about, as long as it is outwardly focused. In that regard, it allows for a great deal of personalization and individualization.

Below are a series of examples outlining what Points of Intersection can look like for a selection of people who represent a wide spectrum of talents, interests, and needs.

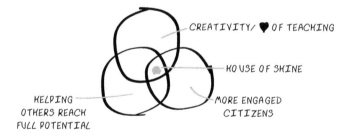

POINT OF INTERSECTION
CLAUDIA, FOUNDER HOUSE OF SHINE

CREATIVITY/ ♥ OF TEACHING

HOUSE OF SHINE

HELPING OTHERS REACH FULL POTENTIAL

MORE ENGAGED CITIZENS

Claudia

Yes, that's me. My journey is a good first example. Creating House of Shine was the perfect nexus of my talents and interests, and a need I saw in my community. The job is big enough that it requires use of all my talents, but at the forefront are my creativity and my love of teaching. My interests center on helping people reach their fullest potential, and the need in my community I most wished to fill that of engendering a more engaged citizenry. My orienting question was this: How do we replace disengaged citizens with communities of people who are motivated to lead and to solve problems that matter?

For me, the POI for those three things is House of Shine. The idea was to create an organization focused on mobilizing people by unearthing and then unleashing their greatest talents and gifts. Because the organization is born out of my Shine, doing the work is immensely fulfilling. The joy I derive by leading this organization and the benefit the work provides to the community creates a virtuous cycle.

Toni

POINT OF INTERSECTION
GRANDMA, ANNUAL CAUSE TRIP

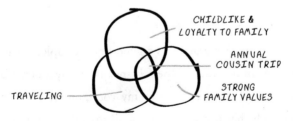

TRAVELING

CHILDLIKE &
LOYALTY TO FAMILY

ANNUAL
COUSIN TRIP

STRONG
FAMILY VALUES

What about something smaller scale; so small-scale it revolves around a single family? My mother-in-law possesses many attributes, not least of which is her skill and thoughtfulness in acting as a mentor to me and her loving assertiveness in giving me a swift kick in the behind when she believes I am not thinking big enough. But she is also a feisty Italian woman who is fiercely committed to her family, loves art, hates losing, and is childlike enough that she is always up for the next great adventure.

She has fulfilled many Points of Intersection during her lifetime, but it is an experience she initiated in her retirement that will undoubtedly be one of her greatest legacies. It's the Cousin Trip, an annual weekend trip designed for her to spend with her eight grandkids. The cousins mark their calendars and then get busy selecting their destination, along with all the attractions they will visit along the way. So far they have visited many cities, including Orlando, San Francisco, Boston, and Philadelphia.

Toni's talents are her childlike nature and her fierce loyalty to her family. Her interests are in traveling and the need her contribution fills is instilling the importance of family into this next generation. The Cousin Trip is responsible for countless family memories and is a beautiful illustration of how even small and local needs can be filled when someone decides to intentionally share her talents and interests.

Sangetta

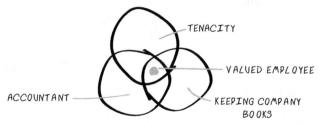

POINT OF INTERSECTION
3ANGEETA,
CORPORATE ACCOUNTING MANAGER

TENACITY

VALUED EMPLOYEE

ACCOUNTANT

KEEPING COMPANY
BOOK3

Now let's look at something larger in scale, a midsize business. Sangetta is an accounting manager who reports to a chief financial officer. She enjoys kidding among her colleagues about being the one person, including the CEO, you don't want searching for you in the hallways. If she is, chances are it is because your expense report is off (even by a few cents), or she has a suggestion about how your department can save dollars here and there.

Colleagues agree Sangetta's talents are the tenacity with which she does her work and the sense of ownership she feels towards the company's financial solvency. She has a genuine interest in accounting, along with formal training, and she fills the critical need of paying the bills and keeping staff in accordance with good accounting practices.

Sangetta's POI seems simple, yet it isn't. All it takes is one bad hire (and one late payroll) to realize what a gift it is to hire someone who shines at her job. When a person's talents and interests align with the needs of her position, she is most likely operating from her natural Point of Intersection and she almost can't help but shine at her job.

Amareesa

POINT OF INTERSECTION
AMAREESA,
HIGH SCHOOL STUDENT

Scaling up further, let's look at how a sophomore in high school used her POI to help at-risk teen girls learn the benefits of journaling.

We at House of Shine first met Amareesa while we were teaching a Problems and Solutions class to tenth-grade students at a local high school. This class was designed to help students identify problems they cared about so that they could complete a year-long project researching and developing solutions to a social problem of their choice. House of Shine curriculum guides students through an exploratory process resulting in projects that are meaningful and not just rote exercises in checking obligatory boxes. During one of our class periods, my colleague and I caught a glimpse of Amareesa's journal after we asked students to reflect on their feelings about a prompt.

Her journal was nothing less than a work of art. The colors, her perfectly scripted fonts, and the artifacts carefully fixed in place with colorful tape were all a feast for the eyes of anyone with a penchant for either creativity or organization (or both). We arranged a lunch date with Amareesa so we could learn the origin of her inspiration. She shared with us that she was creative, but the real reason she journaled was because it allowed her to manage stress and anxiety.

At the time, House of Shine was delving deeper into teaching journaling classes as a way of encouraging young people to spend time in reflection. We recognized a link between reflection, greater self-awareness, and reaching your fullest potential, so hosting formalized journaling classes filled a need we were eager to address. Inviting Amareesa to participate in this initiative seemed like a natural thing to do.

We reworked the classes and trained Amareesa to make her the face of our teachings. We learned that adolescent girls loved the relatability of a high school student sharing how she benefited from her journaling practice, and they were captivated by all the crafty tips and tricks she shared about colors, fonts, and decorative ways to record mundane information. Registration numbers for our workshops increased and Amareesa grew more confident with every session she conducted. Three years later it is easy to see how teaching journaling classes was the perfect Point of Intersection for Amareesa's talents, interests, and a need in our community. Her talent is her creativity, her interest is exploring how journaling helps her positively manage her life, and the need only Amareesa could fill was to make journaling relatable and accessible to more teen girls.

Abigail

POINT OF INTERSECTION
ABIGAIL, BOOK AUTHOR

Now let's go younger in age, but bigger in scope, proving that capacity for making a difference is only limited by our perception of what is possible: My staff and I first met nine-year-old

Abigail Perez at a mother-daughter book event we hosted, with author Margo Manhattan. The featured book, *Follow Your Star*, tells the story of how main character Margo's lifelong love of gems led her to the path she's on today as a well-respected jewelry designer in New York City.

Abigail and her mother attended, less because they are into glitz and glam and more because Abigail has wanted to be a writer since she was four years old. When she arrived at the event she had three books with her, all handwritten and illustrated by Abigail herself. The working title of one was *Super A* and it featured a young girl whose superpower was helping other kids discover their own superpowers.

The idea for *Super A* emanated from experiences Abigail had being bullied in school. Knowing Abigail, it's hard to believe she was bullied—her fine features and soft-spoken nature seem nothing short of angelic. However, kids (like adults) find a way, so the teasing revolved around the healthy lunches Abigail brought to school.

Abigail's belief is that everyone has a superpower and sometimes those powers have nothing to do with brute strength but are about being kind, being a great listener, or trying hard. Her talents involve her caring nature, her love of writing, and her strong work ethic. Her interest is in redefining what it means to be a superhero, and the need she is filling is to craft a relatable message for kids about making positive life choices. Abigail's POI has manifested in her own published book: *How to Be a Super Kid.*

Experiment with your Point of Intersection. Using the concentric circles below, plot your talents and interests, and the needs you see around you. Then try to identify what contribution sits in the middle. Situate within these circles your past contributions or accomplishments, and then try envisioning one for your future. Starting with a past accomplishment can help because this exercise focuses you on a time in your life when something you did was successful. By this point in the book, hopefully you are beginning to see that the reason for your success was that you brought your talents and interests together to fill some sort of need. In the same way we can deconstruct our favorite recipe or craft to identify all the ingredients included, we can also deconstruct our past successes to understand all the things that made it work. When you become better at understanding what made you successful in the past, the better you will get at plotting out potential future opportunities.

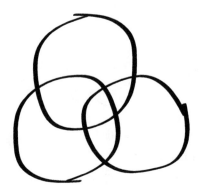

It is important to remember
that the Point of Intersection
grows and changes with us
over time.

While generally my core talents and interests have remained
the same throughout my life, they have also grown and
matured with me. When I was a kid gifted with creativity and an interest in human development, it manifested in
experiences such as being a camp counselor, helping neigh-
bors choreograph a gymnastics routine, and playing school
with my best friend. At college and then graduate school,
those same talents and interests became refined and manifested in more mature ways. During those years, I worked

in Residence Life and planned building-wide programs for students living on campus. I was able to apply my creativity and interest in human development with a newfound interest in community development, eventually publishing a community development model for use on college campuses. And at this time in my life, I find that the way I apply my talents and interests today has changed yet again. My core talents and interests around creativity and human development have remained somewhat constant, but the application continues to grow with me. The same will be true for you.

That's what makes the Shine Method so useful. The principles with which it is built are simple and intuitive: Know who you are through exploration of your Shine; cultivate those qualities that make you unique; and find a corner of the world that needs what you have to offer. These universal principles apply to any situation and they transcend all divisions: age, race, sex, socioeconomic status, location, ability level, and so on. Master those nuggets and you have a framework you can apply for a lifetime that will help you realize fulfillment and success.

If you look around the world at all your favorite products, books, music, pieces of art, bosses, organizations, and people who inspire you, the specialness you notice began with a single person finding his or her Point of Intersection. They did the personal work required to understand their talents, to know their interests, and to recognize opportunities where they could apply them. Steve Jobs did it when he combined his love of design with his interest in technology and the need he saw early on for all people to own personal computers. The entrepreneur down the street from me did it when she combined her business savvy with her interest in cooking and filled a need by providing personal chef services to busy families. And my son found his POI when he figured out how to use his creativity and interest in pottery to help purchase computers for kids who otherwise couldn't afford them. He makes and sells pottery through Jack Pot Ceramics, and donates a portion of his proceeds to a local organization that sells inexpensive refurbished computers to students who need them. Through the Shine Method, it is possible for all people to find their Point of Intersection.

Now What?
Making Your Way In The World

I wrote this book for you as my way of adding another name to House of Shine's growing list of people who are helping to power the planet with Shine. So what's next? Start by using what you've read here to examine what you've come to know about yourself and whether the time you are spending in your daily life is in keeping with what you care about and what the world needs. Only you know whether your local schools or government could benefit from something you have to offer. Or whether the street you live on or state you live in could be inspired to change if you were vulnerable and said "yes" to the idea in your head. It's one book in the hands of one person, but it is rooted in a deep-seated belief that within you are many contributions worth making.

Raindrops hitting the bay outside my window as I write this are evidence that one drop can create a ripple that is felt far and wide. One book in the hands of one person (that's you!) might result in one change, but that one change will make ripples that are felt by many more. And when you share your book (and your favorite tips for journaling) with an entire book club, office, or team, inviting them to invest time in applying the Shine Method to their own lives, the change in whole communities can be exponential.

So where do we go from here? How do we take the ideas shared in this book and apply them to our lives? Central to successfully applying the concepts contained within these pages is realizing that shining is a daily practice. It's a commitment we make each morning when we wake up and not a switch we flip one time when we are feeling especially motivated. The daily practice is, essentially, one of noticing; noticing when you're feeling your best versus when you're feeling sapped of energy. It's being honest with yourself about why you're staying put in a less-than-perfect situation and finding a group of peers who help you feel courageous, not complacent. The practice is most likely to take root in people whose mindset is open to lifelong learning—a continuous cycle of action and reflection.

Scientists exemplify the dedication to ongoing inquiry. Being a scientist is as much a mindset as a vocation; they have a strong commitment and drive to explore their chosen fields of study. In examining your life, it can be helpful and even inspiring to cast yourself in a similar light. In the next section you'll see why I consider you to be a scientist of the most important kind: a Shineologist...

Shineology: The Study of Self; or, What Do I Do from Here?

There isn't an area of scientific study that doesn't have an "-ology" and the study of self should be no different. Anthropology, biology, paleontology, dendrology; all of these are disciplines of science, designed to stimulate our curiosity and to find out why things happen the way they do. We have coined the term "Shineology" to describe the study of self. Engaging with the self, just as in other sciences, means following methods of enquiry and investigating data in order to stimulate creative ideas about how what is learned might be applied.

If Shineology is the study of self, then Shineologists are people who are engaged in this form of enquiry. You, by virtue of reading and participating in some of the activities included in this book, are a Shineologist. Each "-ology" has its own field of study. Anthropologists investigate artifacts as a way of learning about culture. Botanists study plants to learn more about how and why they grow as they do, and in different environments. And paleontologists study fossils to understand the history of life on Earth. Scientists might focus on different fields of study, but they have one thing in common—they follow the scientific method when researching a topic about which they want to know more.

As Shineologists, we record data about our Shine (strengths, hobbies, interests and irritants, needs, and life experiences), then synthesize this information and draw conclusions from it about everything from the work environment we would most enjoy, to patterns in our behavior, to simple likes and dislikes. Shine Notes are a Shineologist's version of a scientist's field notes. The thirty-page journals we designed for K-12 students provide space in which they can write, sketch, or tape material, to track whatever is important to them during that year. Items people have collected include things such as favorite fashion pictures cut out of catalogs; ticket stubs from movies, concerts, or sporting events;

receipts from notable purchases, like a computer or phone; favorite quotes or memes; a graded assignment or report card; stickers or postcards commemorating places traveled; and trackers for information such as hours slept, daily mood, exercise per week, books read, or time spent on social media. Ideas for data that they can capture in their Shine Notes are limited only by the number of ideas they can come up with (and how to make them work in two dimensions). When a year's worth of experiences are captured inside a single journal, then, like a dendrologist who studies rings of a tree trunk to understand the tree's history, students can look back over their annual Shine Notes to better understand themselves.

ANOTHER YEAR, ANOTHER RING

There is a saying that goes, "One is a dot, two is a line, three is a trend." I love that quote as a way of underscoring, again, the philosophy behind capturing Shine Notes and treating each year's journal as a ring in a tree. One entry in the journal is nice and two will be fun to look at, but when we start to see repeated themes three and four times, and spread out over years, we can gain insights into our tendencies in thinking, feeling, and behaving. That information can be immensely helpful as people get older and want to look back on who they were to make informed and decisions about the future they want to craft. While a Shine Notes journal is not essential, we suggest all Shineologists keep a journal of some sort.

Fast-forward a year. What story would the pages of this year's journal tell about you? Would there be answers to any of the questions posed in this book? Would there be evidence of any Shine Workouts that you did, hoping to grow your Shine Muscles? Would your world have expanded by way of people or opportunities as a result of trying to find your Point of Intersection?

Perhaps even more important, if we examined the pages of your journal five or ten more years from now, what would the rings of your life reveal? What common themes would we find? What project would you be working on that we could date back to entries from two or three years earlier? What kinds of similarities and differences would you see in your strengths, hobbies, interests and irritants, needs, and experiences? What Points of Intersection might you have discovered?

It's never too late to feed the roots; to carve out short periods of time each week to get to know yourself better through reflection and data gathering. The practice will prove to be an energy and growth source in the same way photosynthesis is an energy and growth source for trees. Your growing self-awareness will shed new light on old ways of being and with that knowledge you will be able to convert what you know about who you are and why this matters into a fulfilling and flourishing life.

Now get to it. Turn over a new leaf and decide you're going to branch out.

AFTERWORD

What Is House of Shine?

More than a decade later, House of Shine has evolved from a daily blog to a formalized nonprofit. At House of Shine we share a conviction that inside every person is a contribution waiting to be made. We are motivated by the simple idea that the world would be a better place if every person was actively engaged in making it so. Our work is fueled by years of positive psychology research that asserts that people are happier and more fulfilled when they are using their strengths to help other people. Normalizing this virtuous cycle of giving and receiving is central to our mission, and it is House of Shine's upstream solution to helping ward off a series of downstream problems ranging from bullying to teen mental health challenges, to lagging employee and civic engagement.

We assert that unearthing a person's unique combination of talents and gifts, as well as helping them see the utility of those attributes, requires self-awareness. We organize the process of self-discovery inside a framework called the Shine Method. People explore their strengths, hobbies, interests and irritants, needs, and experiences, and then use that information to find a Point of Intersection (POI). The POI is the sweet spot—the point of convergence among a person's talents, interests, and a need in world they would like to help fill. All the offerings provided by House of Shine are meant to facilitate this self-discovery.

Simon Sinek introduced the world to the concept of "The Golden Circle" in his book *Start with Why*. He observed, in discussing this concept, that the most successful organizations created inspired work by starting with their "why"—the core belief that draws users in emotionally. Only then do these organizations spend time talking about how to meet their brand promise and, ultimately, what widget it is they will produce or manufacture. We found this concept immensely useful in helping other people understand the work of House of Shine.

Why

Communities are only as strong as the involvement of those living in them. From schools to workplaces, to community organizations, and even voter turnout, when people do not feel connected to the communities in which they live, they are less invested and less likely to participate. Conversely, when people view themselves as integral members of their community—as having something to offer and contribute—they are happier, more confident, and more likely to get involved. With feelings of isolation, anxiety, and depression are on the rise, it is more important than ever to teach people how to extrapolate talents and gifts from previous life experiences and use them to connect with their communities.

How

The way we instill a sense of contribution in people is by unearthing their unique combination of talents and gifts, then helping people imagine how sharing those things can improve some corner of their world. This corner can be as small as a single family, a classroom, or a team, or it can be as big as a regional, national, or international initiative. The size and scale of a person's contribution is determined by the individual himself and, of course, it can change over time. We use the acronym "SHINE" to guide people's self-exploration: S=Strengths, H=Hobbies, I=Interests and Irritants, N=Needs, and E=Experiences.

At a time when the world is getting noisier and external messages about what is prized and valued are getting louder and louder, an explicit invitation for people of all ages to stop, think, and reflect on the core of who they are is more important than ever.

What

Few of us would get in a car today without a map or navigational system to help us get from point A to point B. House of Shine envisions itself as providing the navigational tools a person needs to find purpose and direction—a way to get from their point A to their point B. How do we do it? Our team develops experiential teaching tools and programs that facilitate self-reflection and conversation about some of life's most important questions: Who am I and why does this matter?

Specifically, we write curriculum for kids K-12, offer school assemblies, summer camps, weekend workshops, evening classes for adults and parents, monthly workshops for women, and corporate training sessions. Additionally, we publish a blog, host a podcast, and have developed a collection of teaching tools people can purchase to use on their own.

THE GOLDEN CIRCLE

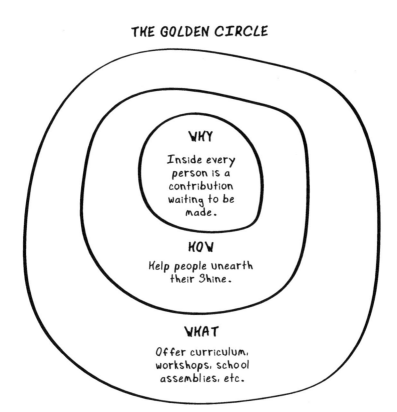

WHY

Inside every person is a contribution waiting to be made.

HOW

Help people unearth their Shine.

WHAT

Offer curriculum, workshops, school assemblies, etc.

CONCEPT BY SIMON SINEK

CPSIA information can be obtained
at www.ICGtesting.com
Printed in the USA
LVHW051922091221
705683LV00003B/18/J

9 780578 614731